CURRICULUM IMPROVEMENT:

An Administrator's Guide

CURRICULUM IMPROVEMENT:
An Administrator's Guide

George G. Tankard, Jr.

Parker Publishing Company, Inc.
West Nyack, N. Y.

Library of Congress Cataloging in Publication Data

Tankard, George Granville,
    Curriculum improvement.

    Bibliography: p.
    1. Curriculum planning--Handbooks, manuals, etc.
I. Title.
LB1570.T22   375'.001   74-13123
ISBN 0-13-195917-4

Printed in the United States of America

DEDICATION

With respect and humility I dedicate this book to my
parents, Mr. and Mrs. George Tankard, Sr., and to my
mother-in-law, Mrs. Wallace J. Wiseman—all living
testimony to the fact that there doesn't have to be a
generation gap.

Your Guide to On-Going Curriculum Improvement

This book is written for the front line school administrator, and it will serve as an invaluable handbook for those who are faced with the need to bring about curriculum improvement. It offers realistic guidance on how to get the curriculum from where it is to where it ought to be. As such it can be used in two ways: (1) as the basis for developing a total plan for curriculum improvement, or (2) as a ready reference guide for making progress on specific aspects of the improvement process.

As an on-the-job educator, you are currently attempting to meet the demands of education's critics; and, at the same time, trying to provide improved education for youngsters. This book will:

(1) Give you, in practical, everyday language a review of current procedures for bringing about curriculum improvement.

(2) Present plans that you may adopt or easily adapt to meet the needs in your school district.

(3) Provide specific suggestions on how to best use available personnel in the curriculum improvement process.

(4) Supply guidance in critical areas such as communications, community involvement, financing, staffing, organization, and evaluation.

(5) Provide you with actual samples of forms, check lists, evaluation guides, schedules and procedural outlines.

While the book takes into account various aspects of changes and conceptual models for effecting change, its primary emphasis is upon practical programs and techniques that have actually been field tested. The conclusions and recommendations are based upon the degree of success achieved by tested approaches.

The material falls into several categories. First, an analysis of current practice has been included to provide a strong basis for developing the strategy for curriculum improvement. Selected current approaches, together with the strengths and limitations of each are reviewed in non-technical language. The characteristics of a potentially effective approach are identified to provide a model for use in your school district. Emphasis is placed upon the procedures for planning and implementing a curriculum improvement program and Chapter 3 provides a schedule of the essential steps in the process.

Since people on your staff are the key to curriculum improvement, Chapters 5-9 deal with the appropriate utilization of staff and other persons. Included are specific guidelines for the superintendent, principal, teachers, other staff members, pupils, members of the board of education, and outside resource people. Guides for establishing salaries, classifications, and working arrangements are given. Procedures for improving communications, orientation, level of participation, job satisfaction, professional growth, and acceptance of change during the curriculum improvement process are outlined. Guidelines are provided for working with parents and citizen groups. Procedures for organizing and staffing are included and coordination with existing programs is described.

Case histories involving a systematic approach to curriculum improvement are discussed in detail in Chapter 10. Based upon the successes and failures of currently operating programs, this chapter outlines the steps in planning, developing, and implementing curriculum improvement projects, together with guidelines for decision making. It provides an experience-based plan against which you may compare your improvement programs, both current and anticipated.

And finally, the remaining chapters deal with specific aspects of the curriculum improvement area. Included are guidelines for developing instructional materials, financing the improvement program, and evaluating the curriculum improvement plan. Also included are discussions of budgeting, data processing, PPBES, and various techniques to determine effectiveness.

The final chapter underscores the fact that quality education is attainable only through continuous curriculum improvement.

You will find this a manual for the curriculum innovator. It is action oriented and experience validated. It is full of do's and don'ts drawn from field experience and includes techniques to be used in the curriculum improvement process. Selective listings of resource materials are included. It is intended for you, the experienced on-the-job educator. We believe you will find it a most useful manual and guide for curriculum improvement.

George G. Tankard, Jr.

ACKNOWLEDGEMENTS

Many persons with specialized knowledge and experience have assisted me in the preparation of *Curriculum Improvement: An Administrator's Guide.* I wish to acknowledge the contributions and advice received from George Hamel, Harold Hodge, Larry Byers, Frank Moore, and Ronald Dearden—all of the Fairfax County Public Schools, for their preparation, respectively, of the initial draft of the chapters on communications, school staff, financing, materials, and evaluation; and to thank S. John Davis, Superintendent of Fairfax County Schools, for providing many of the forms and illustrative activities used throughout the book. To Herb Shelley, long time friend and retired elementary school principal, go my thanks for assistance in preparing the original outline and reviewing the final manuscript; and to Betty Miller goes an accolade for preparing a readable, usable manuscript.

A special debt of gratitude goes to Roger W. Webb, also of the Fairfax County Schools who worked closely with me in developing, organizing, and editing the final manuscript, and who prepared the chapters on the current approaches to curriculum improvement and the educational systems approach. Without Roger's invaluable assistance and support a readable manuscript by the publisher's deadlines would never have materialized. His many suggestions for improvement and his countless hours of detailed review are sincerely appreciated.

Last, but certainly not least, thanks to my family—to my wife, Madeline, and to Mary and Buddy. Without Madeline's typing and retyping of my rough notes and without her persistence, friendly but firm, I might never have finished the book. Mary's and Buddy's interest, support, and patience helped tremendously. Most important of all, they provided the real reason for attempting the task in the first place.

Contents

11

1

Determining What
Needs Improving

The first step in the curriculum improvement cycle is the identification of the curriculum area to be improved. In most instances, several areas can be identified as needing improvement and warranting special attention and additional resources. The administrator must determine which areas of the program need attention, how badly they need it, and assign priorities for attention accordingly.

Meeting identified needs of pupils and community should be the basis for curriculum change and improvement. In fact, we might argue that a change that does not meet a need, or meet a need better, is really not an improvement at all or, at best, is an unnecessary improvement. Changes take three forms: the addition of something new; the deletion of something in existence; or the alteration and modification of something in existence. The administrator and the community have to go from that uneasy feeling that "all is not well" to a clear identification of what should be added to, deleted from, or changed in the present educational program. This is the first step in the curriculum improvement process which is discussed throughout this book and is the major theme of this chapter.

How do we make these decisions? How do we decide what to add, what to drop, and what to keep and try to improve?

Historically, and all too often in present practice, pressures such as the following have led to curriculum change: competition with Russia and Sputnik, community pressure, forceful salesmen, political expediency, enthusiasm of a given staff member, "everybody's doing it," availability of Federal funds, or the influence of a school board member. This list will go on and on unless a school or school system develops a systematic, rational way of assessing its needs and planning its improvements.

The administrator must accept the fact that the meeting of pupil and community needs is the most valid basis for selecting areas for curriculum improvement. He should accept the thesis that education is quality education to the extent that needs are met effectively, efficiently, and satisfactorily. He should then draw upon the variety of instruments and techniques at hand for identifying these needs and developing a systematic program for meeting them.

The establishing of these needs should take place in four steps:

(1) assessing the existing program—objectives, content, and effectiveness,
(2) establishing of the total needs of pupils and community,
(3) determining unmet needs by comparing the total needs with those being met by the existing program, and
(4) selecting specific area(s) for improvements.

ASSESSING THE EXISTING PROGRAM

Objectives

A clear, concise statement of the objectives of the school and/or school system should be available. Many times such a statement has not been developed or is too vague or general. If objectives have been written, they can usually be found in publications or course guides for the district or in the various reports prepared by the individual schools. Current literature provides valuable assistance, and source materials are cited throughout this book. If a statement of objectives is not available, the preparation of such a statement is the first step in the process.

Content

The content of the program is usually described in course outlines, lists of high school offerings, accreditation reports, state reports, and other written materials. If your district does not have such descriptions in a single document, an important initial step is to compile one, and make it available to all concerned.

Effectiveness

The effectiveness of the program can be assessed through three types of performance measures:

(1) scores on standardized tests of mental ability, subject matter readiness, subject matter achievement, vocational skill achievement, etc.
(2) school attendance, grade completion, number of dropouts, summer school enrollments, physical performance and defects, age-grade distribution, etc.
(3) postgraduate and follow-up measures such as further study, number completing, vocational placement, beginning salaries, etc.

If your school system does not have such an analysis of its present operation, much of the remainder of this book will be rather useless to you. Take immediate steps to prepare such a descriptive profile of your school or district.

ESTABLISHING PUPIL AND COMMUNITY NEEDS

In addition to an analysis of the present program, an assessment of pupil and community needs must be made. Once again, most of the information needed is available. It simply needs to be organized and presented in an orderly fashion. Many nonschool agencies, both private and public, are ready to assist and should be utilized.

The following resources and procedures can be utilized in the identification of needs:

(1) Existing data and written material

(2) Research and study by administrative and supervisory staff
(3) Teacher participation
(4) Student participation
(5) Accreditation and self-study reports
(6) State mandated accountability and/or quality standards
(7) Board of Education
(8) Citizen task forces and advisory committee reports
(9) The comprehensive community survey
(10) The single purpose survey
(11) Outside consultants

In fact, any total plan should be developed utilizing any or all of these, in varying degrees, depending upon the situation. Also, any of those listed will draw heavily on others if effectively done. They are discussed individually for clarity of presentation.

(1) Existing Data and Written Material

Most of the data necessary to establish pupil needs and to determine the extent to which these needs are being met are available. They simply need to be collected, organized, and clearly presented. The following list of data sources will be utilized in most of the techniques discussed in this chapter. They are listed here to serve as a resource guide regardless of which purpose(s) they may have. Names may vary and few localities will have them all.

LOCAL DATA SOURCES

School

Official School Records
Publications of School District
Test Scores
Superintendent's Annual Report
Drop-out Statistics
Follow-up Studies of Graduates and Dropouts
Annual School Budget
School Census
Research Publications

Special Education Data
Local Education Association Publications

Nonschool

Department of Research and Planning
Police Department
Department of Economic Development (by whatever name)
Welfare Department
Public Information and Research Office
Citizen Advisory Commissions
Local Universities
Park and Recreation Agencies
Court Records
Local Real Estate Association
Chamber of Commerce
Public Utilities
Private School Groups
Individual Citizens
Private Consultant Organizations

STATE, FEDERAL, AND REGIONAL DATA SOURCES

Department of Education
Department of Planning and Finance
Department of Taxation
Bureau of the Census
U.S. Office of Education
Professional Organizations—AASA, NEA, ASCD, ACEI, AESP, NASSP, ABSO, NSSE, etc.
State Education Association

(2) Research and Study by Administrative and Supervisory Staff

The staff of the school or school system should be assessing the needs of the pupils and community on a continuing basis. This should be done in an orderly, systematic fashion. Statistical and descriptive data should be maintained to:

(1) provide historical perspective,
(2) identify established trends,
(3) point to needed changes,

(4) assist in budgeting and allocation of resources, and

(5) support new requests for resources.

In addition to base data being collected it may be necessary to do much more comprehensive indentification of needs and weaknesses to support major moves toward curriculum improvement. This may be done by:

(1) utilizing existing research, planning and evaluation personnel if they are available,

(2) reassigning and changing work emphasis of existing personnel,

(3) creating a special study group or task force group from existing staff, or

(4) a combination of these.

It is the responsibility of superintendent, principals, and staff to see that existing data are fully utilized in the curriculum improvement process and are made available to all groups concerned. This responsibility must not go to those outside the school system, either by intent or default.

(3) Teacher Participation

The participation and contributions of teachers are essential to the needs assessment process. Teachers from all appropriate disciplines and levels of instruction should be involved and should participate during the entire process. The role of the school staff in the entire curriculum improvement process is discussed in Chapter 6.

(4) Student Participation

Students at all levels should be involved in the needs assessment process. The administrator must provide a means for their thoughts and evaluation of the existing program to be a part of curriculum evaluation and improvement. They must be involved in all stages of the process. The role of students in the entire curriculum improvement process is discussed in Chapter 8.

(5) Accreditation and Self-Study Reports

Virtually all secondary schools and many elementary schools in this country are accredited by state and/or regional accrediting agencies. Most accreditation studies and reports include the identification of weak and strong areas in the school, and recommended steps for improvement. The school principal should use such a study as an opportunity to assess the instructional needs in his school. The superintendent should see that these studies are not forgotten but serve as the basis for planned improvement. All too often they are filed away with a sigh of relief once the school is accredited.

In a large school system these studies can be analyzed and summarized to:

(1) identify common needs throughout the school system,
(2) identify the composition of the community served,
(3) pinpoint needs unique to a single school,
(4) assist in the allocation of special resources,
(5) determine the need for various types of personnel, and
(6) determine broad goals.

If these reports are to be compiled and analyzed, attention should be given in advance to the form in which data will be collected so that they will be combinable and statistically usable. This is often possible with secondary reports, with their detail of course offerings, class sizes, etc.; but frequently not possible at the elementary level. When these reports deal largely with courses, objectives, resources available, class size, buildings, and equipment, limitations are imposed upon the usefulness of the information. The administrator must recognize these limitations and may need to devise a means of collecting additional information about changes in pupils.

(6) State Mandated Accountability and/or Quality Standards

Many states have, or are in the process of legislating, accountability standards for public education. Usually this legislation establishes standards to be met, requires local school districts to work toward these standards, requires assessment of the extent to which these standards are being met, and may provide for a review and penalty for those failing to meet these standards. This usually requires an assessment of current programs and levels of support to establish a baseline against which to measure performance. Any such legislation or state directive, either in effect or anticipated, should be used as a vehicle for needs assessment.

(7) Board of Education

The local board of education must be involved in the assessment plan. They should be involved early, given a chance to contribute, and an opportunity to react, modify and improve. The administrator should utilize the expertise and interest of the board, both as a body and as individuals. The role of the board of education is discussed in Chapter 9.

(8) Citizen Task Forces and Advisory Committee Reports

Citizen groups may be used as single purpose task forces or continuing advisory committees. A task force to develop long-range community recreational, educational, and cultural goals and a continuing advisory committee for vocational education have been quite effective in Fairfax City, Virginia, and Fairfax County, Virginia respectively. A detailed discussion of the utilization of citizen groups is found in Chapter 9.

(9) The Comprehensive Community Survey

The comprehensive community survey consists of a detailed

survey of all the cultural, recreational, and educational resources in the community. It may be conducted by the school staff, a combination of all governmental agencies concerned, outside consultants, or any combination of these. It may or may not make specific recommendations, depending upon its purpose.

Such a survey should contain:

(1) An introduction explaining its purpose, by whom authorized and supported, the method of preparation, and the future steps planned.
(2) A general description of the community including its history and geography; its education, economic, and cultural resources; its income and financial condition; and its form of government.
(3) A description of its public school system—including vocational programs, its instructional support activities, and supporting services.
(4) Other educational, cultural, and recreation resources in the community such as private schools, higher education, parks, libraries, mental health activities, etc.

The table of contents from such a study is shown as Figure 1-1 for illustrative purposes.[1]

(10) The Single Purpose Survey

It may be desirable to conduct a short, single purpose survey in an attempt to obtain specific information or to obtain a sampling of citizens' opinion. Such a survey should be limited to a few questions with its purpose carefully explained to the community and with its results made available to the public. In some instances this may be made a part of some regularly conducted poll such as the school census. A copy of such a survey form used for recreational planning is included as Figure 1-2.

(11) Outside Consultants

Outside consultants may be employed to assist in the identification of pupil needs. This may be part of a total survey of the

---

[1]Fairfax County Public Schools, Title III Planning Staff, *A Basic Survey of Fairfax County, It's Educational and Cultural Resources.*

Figure 1-1

FAIRFAX CITY SCHOOL CENSUS
Spring 1973   Team_____

School_____

NAME_____

ADDRESS_____

CHILD'S NAME	DATE OF BIRTH	AGE	SEX	SCHOOL (Check one)			
				Public	Private	College	None

1. How many adults participated in adult education/ recreation programs offered by the city or county during the past 12 months?

County locations _____

City locations _____

2. How many children participated in the city volunteer athletic programs during the past twelve months?

Boys _____   Girls _____

Ages_____|_____

3. In what other non-school activities conducted in city or county schools do your children participate? (e.g., Scouts, choral groups, square dancing, etc.)

_____
_____
_____

4. What recreational and cultural activities, not presently provided at the Fairfax High School or other city locations, would your family participate in if available in the city?

1._____
2._____
3._____

5. What improvements or additions in facilities would you like to see most at Lanier and the elementary school serving your area?

1._____
2._____
3._____

6. From the following list, indicate three facilities that your family would use if available, in order of preference. (Use "None" or "Others" as appropriate)
   (a) a city aquatic center (swimming pool),
   (b) a community center to include a small auditorium and little theater,
   (c) gymnasium space for youth and adult basketball, probably located at existing schools,
   (d) Expanded community facilities such as meeting places, handball courts, additional tennis courts, etc., at existing elementary schools,
   (e) bicycle paths,
   (f) none of these,
   (g) others (specify)

1._____

2._____

3._____

Figure 1-2

school system or an independent study of the instructional program. Such a study may be done by university and college personnel, state department of education personnel, or private consultants. The task of such consultants usually includes the recommendation of remedies as well as the identification of needs. The use of outside resources is covered in Chapter 9.

DETERMINING UNMET NEEDS

Once the existing program has been assessed and the total needs of the pupils and community have been established, unmet needs must be identified using the following formula:

TOTAL NEEDS *minus* NEEDS BEING ADEQUATELY
MET BY EXISTING PROGRAM *equal* UNMET NEEDS

The list provides the shopping list from which improvement projects should be drawn. The final step in the process becomes the establishing of priorities.

The following statements represent actual needs identified by selected schools in Fairfax County, Virginia:

(1) Analysis of math achievement test scores indicates a need to increase proficiency in math computation skills.
(2) A staff survey indicates the need for improving interpersonal relationships among teachers and within the community.
(3) Evaluation of student written work and study of standardized aptitude and achievement test scores indicate that expository writing is not at a level appropriate to ability and needs of the students.
(4) Although more students receive satisfactory ratings on the physical fitness test each year, they continue to score substantially lower on items involving strength and agility than in other areas.
(5) Staff analysis of the program for hearing-impaired children indicates assistance is needed in curriculum development, guidance for parents for follow-up instruction, inservice programs for teachers, and coordination between special education services and the school.
(6) After a study of test scores and a consensus of faculty discussion, the main program focus will continue to be the development of quality in the communicative and computative skills.
(7) There is continued concern about general progress and achievement in

the skill areas of language arts (particularly reading), arithmetic, and problem solving. A number of the teaching staff showed the need for upgrading in the area of media techniques.

(8) The present student body appears to justify an increase in vocational offerings.

SELECTING THE SPECIFIC AREAS FOR IMPROVEMENT

Any conscientious and thorough assessment of needs will usually result in the identification of many more desirable improvements than the financial, personnel and time resources will support. The areas for emphasis will have to be a combination of what is mandated, what is pressured, and what a needs assessment identifies. However, the following criteria will assist in the selection of those areas to be covered first:

(1) Will the program meet the most critical needs of the population to be served?

(2) Does it show potential for changing pupil behavior?

(3) Is the program within the financial capability of the district?

(4) Is it administratively manageable—are qualified people available? Are program materials available? Is enough time available?

(5) Are the potential results commensurable with the cost, effort, and planning required?

(6) Will disruption to the existing program "cancel out" the gains achieved in the new program?

(7) Will the program have a rippling effect? Will it clear up difficulties or deficiencies that will improve performance in other areas?

(8) Does it address itself specifically to more than one identified need of the group to be served?

(9) Have similar projects elsewhere been studied and visited to profit by other's mistakes?

The answer to all, or most, of these questions except (6) should be "yes" before an area is selected for improvement.

Once areas for improvement have been selected, strategies must be developed for effecting desired improvements. Chapter 2 reviews strategies currently being used throughout the country, and Chapter 3 provides guides to the administrator for planning approaches suited to the needs of his school or district.

2

Current Approaches to Curriculum Improvement

Once an area for curriculum improvement has been identified, the program administrator must select an approach. This chapter examines strengths and weaknesses of current approaches to curriculum improvement.

Approaches to curriculum improvement have taken different forms to serve varied purposes. Efforts to improve curriculum are classified here as:

(1) the authoritarian/directive approach,
(2) the curriculum council/study group approach,
(3) the inservice/staff development approach, and
(4) the educational systems approach.

No approach is either all good or all bad; rather, each approach may be appropriate for certain types of curriculum changes or program improvements. Furthermore, any good curriculum improvement plan probably will contain elements of all four approaches.

Curriculum improvement efforts may focus on a specific content area at a specific grade level or across all grades; they may be targeted at improving the instructional process or they may be concerned with changing the learning environment within a school or schools. The curriculum improvement may be as minor as selecting alternative instructional materials of relatively minor import or as major as the development of a new course of study for inclusion in the total curriculum.

The impetus for curriculum change or improvement may be based on mandates from state and/or regional accrediting agencies; influence from community pressure or special interest groups; an ill-defined sense of a need for change identified by teachers, curriculum specialists, department heads, and administrators; or a well-defined and documented need that has emerged as a result of intensive investigation by staff and community groups.

AUTHORITARIAN/DIRECTIVE APPROACH

The authoritarian or directive approach to curriculum improvement can be distinguished from other approaches in that the impetus for improvement, the direction for improvement, and the focus or target area for improvement are controlled by the program administrator (department head, principal, or district superintendent). Frequently, this approach is used to implement mandated changes that have been imposed by an external agency such as an accrediting or legislative body. This approach is based on a "top-down," paternalistic administrative model which uses the program administrator to expedite a program improvement. Occasionally, this approach is used by an administrator to implement a "pet project" without staff consultation.

Characterized by forceful administrative support of the new or modified program, the curriculum improvement may be legitimized through official adoption of school policy, issuance of regulations and directives enforcing implementation of the program, and budgetary support to ensure that appropriate human and material resources will be made available to undergird the program.

This approach to improvement has the built-in strength of administrative support. Discussion of the pros and cons of the change is minimized, thus expediting the implementation of change. On the negative side, the staff may resent having a predetermined program imposed upon them and thus not be fully or even partially committed to it, and the staff may not possess the knowledge or competencies required for program success. More importantly, changes that are implemented using this approach may not meet the legitimate needs of the school or school district. The negative factors that operate in reaction to the authoritarian approach usually limit its application to rather minor program modifications.

The authoritarian/directive approach may be quite appropriate in those instances where the program changes are minor in nature and will have minor impact on schools, teachers, and students. Major changes in courses of study or instructional procedures will require that the program administrator resort to the curriculum council/study group approach or the inservice/staff development approach.

A clear example of the authoritarian/directive approach can be illustrated by the actions of a state in implementing a new curriculum in health for the elementary grades. Guidelines and textbooks were provided to schools and teachers by the state, and state accreditation requirements were amended to ensure that health would be taught to elementary school children. The program was implemented statewide; however, many of the teachers were ill-prepared to teach health and were forced to rely heavily on the textbooks for guidance, and many teachers were required to make room for another subject in an already over-crowded curriculum. The program was implemented on the assumption that it would improve gradually over the years.

Although the authoritarian/directive approach may not be the most effective approach to ensure quality implementation of major curriculum changes, it does provide an effective vehicle for improvements having the following characteristics:

(1) Improvement is mandated.
(2) Improvement has minor budget implications.
(3) Improvement must be initiated within a strict timetable.
(4) Improvement is minor in nature.
(5) Improvement does not require significant coordination between departments and schools.
(6) Improvement does not require extensive staff training or involvement.

CURRICULUM COUNCIL/STUDY GROUP APPROACH

The curriculum council/study group approach has as its major characteristic the involvement of professional staff members over an extended period of time in an effort to improve the curriculum through study and selection of materials and procedures. School accreditation self-study committees are most commonly of this type, as are districtwide curriculum committees that meet on a regular basis. This approach is based on an administrative model which encourages staff input as a prelude to administrative decision-making.

The inherent value of this approach is the involvement by the teaching staff in the development of recommendations that will affect them in their work. This approach usually assumes that "what we have is good," but that it can be improved. Minor changes can be made over extended periods of time using this approach giving rise to what might be called an evolving curriculum; however, strong leadership may cause major restructuring of the curriculum. Changes usually effected through the curriculum council/study group approach are concerned with modification of program designs, instructional procedures, and alternative materials, equipment, and textbooks.

Among the weaknesses of this approach to curriculum improvements are the following:

(1) a recommended change may not receive support of the program administrator,
(2) the evolutionary nature of change under this approach results in rather minor modifications of the program, whereas decisive change may be necessary in order to make appropriate strides toward meeting the goals of the school or division,
(3) curriculum committees may be too subject- or content-oriented, thereby losing sight of the bigger picture of the needs of the entire school or school division and resulting in fragmented curriculum improvement,
(4) recommended changes may be just changes rather than improvements to the educational program,
(5) study groups may be used as a delaying device to avoid change, and
(6) the curriculum council/study group serves as an ad hoc group, limiting follow-up on implementation or evaluation of changes.

Accreditation self-study provides an example of the study group approach where school faculties examine their programs on the premise that curriculum will be improved through the process. Unfortunately, most of the time devoted to self-studies is at the end of the school day when teachers and administrators are tired. The examination of the educational program and recommendations are faithfully recorded, edited, published, and then often placed on a shelf to be forgotten.

Frequently, curriculum councils are convened to examine new curricular materials and textbooks that have become available. These materials selection committees review and make recommendations regarding the adoption of textbooks and other instructional materials. The fallacy of this approach is that most instructional materials have never been subjected to evaluation in terms of student outcomes or program goals and objectives. Here again, curriculum (in terms of textbooks and instructional materials) may be changed for the sake of change rather than for intentional program improvement.

Project VAL-LEAD[1] (an instructional program designed to develop values, valuing, and leadership) was a three-year, school-based study developed by a curriculum study group composed of administrative, guidance, English, and social studies personnel. This project grew out of the concern that the traditional curriculum in English and social studies was not effectively addressing value development in a time when traditional American values were being challenged in the school community.

The social studies curriculum was designed to help each student understand the reality of himself, of other people in his environment, and of the relationship between himself and the others in his environment. The English segment of the program was centered around the search for identity and appreciation for the rights of others. Extensive courses of study outlining goals, objectives, and selected materials were developed for both the social studies and English portions of the project.

---

[1]Webb, Roger W., *Project VAL-LEAD: An Instructional Program to Develop Values, Valuing, and Leadership,* Fairfax County Public Schools, Fairfax, Virginia, 1970.

The guidance portion was devoted to student self-evaluation, goal setting, and the establishment of realistic patterns of behavior. An essential element of the guidance seminars was planned growth in self-confidence through instruction in techniques of leadership.

Evaluation of the VAL-LEAD project showed that the curriculum and materials selected by the study group were effective in producing positive changes in students' values and leadership characteristics. In this instance, a rather significant program resulted from an interdisciplinary curriculum study group approach.

The curriculum council/study group approach is an effective means for curriculum improvements that have the following characteristics:

(1) Improvements are concerned with minor revisions or modifications of the present curricula.
(2) Staff involvement is necessary for morale purposes and for securing information relative to the present program.
(3) Sufficient time is available to engage in extensive study.
(4) Staff development is not necessarily required by the recommended improvements.
(5) Communication and coordination between departments and schools is deemed essential to the improvement.
(6) Staff assistance in program interpretation and implementation is desired.

INSERVICE/STAFF DEVELOPMENT APPROACH

The inservice/staff development approach adheres to the theory that you must change people and their patterns of operation in order to effect curriculum change. Inherent in this approach is the assumption that the manner in which the staff is presently operating can be improved through seminar or practicum experiences.

Inservice and staff development experiences generally can be divided into those that deal with subject matter or content and those which are primarily concerned with the teacher's role in the instructional process. The major strength in this approach lies in the development of a common understanding among teachers as to the changes in content and their application in the classroom, and the intricacies involved in new or different instructional techniques. The major drawbacks to this approach consist of:

(1) the extensive involvement of staff time and other resources necessary to ensure effective staff development,
(2) the inference that simulated staff development activities can be transferred and applied in actual classroom situations, and
(3) the lack of a built-in system of evaluation to test the effectiveness of the change once it has been implemented in the schools of the district.

The phased-in implementation of a new science curricula for elementary school students by a major school division provides an excellent example of effective use of the staff development approach. This district, moving from a content-oriented science program to one that stressed inquiry, discovery, and the methodology of the scientist required that all teachers who were going to implement the program be involved in intensive staff development activities. Distribution of packaged program materials was controlled by the science program administrator who also served a follow-up function to ensure that the program was properly implemented. Close monitoring of the program ensured that the integrity of the program was held paramount.

Less satisfactory is the following example of an inservice/staff development program designed to alter teaching procedures in the classroom. Extensive staff time during the summer was devoted to modifying instructional techniques in a practicum setting. However, the teacher-pupil ratio was greatly reduced leaving considerable doubt as to the applicability of the new approaches to a *real* classroom setting. Unfortunately, the staff development design did not originally build in a follow-up or evaluation procedure to determine the effectiveness of the training in terms of its practical application.

The inservice/staff development approach may be considered an effective means for curriculum improvements that have the following characteristics:

(1) Improvement represents a major change in curriculum content or instructional procedures.
(2) Improvement requires common understandings among teachers and other staff.
(3) Improvement requires staff training in order to assure appropriate implementation.
(4) Improvement requires a change in staff attitude in order to ensure staff support for the improvement.

EDUCATIONAL SYSTEMS APPROACH

The educational systems approach to curriculum improvement differs sharply from the previously discussed approaches in that it is based on clearly identified and documented educational needs of students. The essential elements of this approach consist of:

(1) specification of the goals and objectives for students of the school or school district,
(2) assessment of the present status of students of the school or district relative to the goals and objectives,
(3) determination of needs (defined as the discrepancy between the performance of students and the goals and objectives),
(4) ranking of needs in terms of their priority and selection of needs for program improvement,
(5) planning a program that will meet these needs,
(6) program implementation
(7) program evaluation in terms of the extent to which program goals and objectives have been met utilizing the new program, and
(8) continuance, modification, or aborting of the program based on evaluative findings.

Inherent in the educational systems approach is the broadbased involvement of administrators, teachers, the school board, public and students.

The educational systems approach is merely a systematic and logical method to facilitate intentional curriculum improvement. Departing from other approaches to improvement, it concentrates on educational products or outcomes of educational programs, i.e., student performances, skills, attitudes, and knowledge.

Instructional means and procedures are considered important to the extent that they contribute to attainment of the program objectives. Its value stems from its emphasis on a needs-based curriculum improvement plan with built-in requirements for evaluation.

Among the drawbacks to the educational systems approach to curriculum improvement are the following:

(1) the extensive involvement of staff and community personnel in planning, implementation, and evaluation;
(2) the concentration on educational products or outcomes that may cause overlooking the importance of the educational process;
(3) the momentum built up through large-scale involvement in planning or extensive study may force untimely implementation or delay implementation indefinitely.

Additional problems in applying the systems approach will be addressed in Chapter 10 where a more extended discussion of the approach is presented.

The educational systems approach requires extensive involvement of staff time and other resources from the initial planning stages through the total implementation of the program improvement. Major program improvements should be pilot-tested and field-tested prior to their blanket implementation. Continual program monitoring, evaluation, and modification (where warranted) provide the necessary safeguards against massive implementation of undesirable program elements. These cautions insure that the program can be modified as necessary for individual schools. Extensive involvement of this nature is essential to the successful application of this approach.

The educational systems approach is an effective means for dealing with major program improvements, especially in large, complex school districts. Staff development and curriculum councils may well be facets of the total plan for educational improvement under the systems approach.

Fairfax County, Virginia has implemented a Planning, Programming, Budgeting, Evaluation System (PPBES) which ties the educational systems approach into the budgetary process. This school division has developed its overall goals or missions, and each school determines on the basis of its unique needs which programs should receive emphasis and budgetary support during the ensuing year. Further consideration will be given to the PPBES approach in Chapter 11.

Another example of the educational systems approach to improvement may be provided by the efforts of a consortium of school districts to provide a third-year general mathematics curriculum for noncollege-bound students. The need for the program was two-fold: first, no such course of study was available for students; and second, students had a two-year gap in the learning and application of certain skills that were necessary in order to improve their employability at the conclusion of their high school experience.

This curriculum improvement project involved master teachers in the development of experimental curriculum materials for the course. Potential teachers were engaged in inservice and staff development activities.

Over a period of three years, the program was pilot tested, field tested, and then made available to all secondary schools in the state. Built-in evaluation of instruction, materials, and student performance was used to incorporate necessary changes into the program.

The educational systems approach provides an effective means for improvements having the following characteristics:

(1) Improvement is of major import and will affect a significant number of teachers, students and administrators.
(2) Improvement requires extensive cooperation between individuals, departments, and schools.
(3) Improvement has logistic complications.
(4) Improvement is based on identified and documented needs.
(5) Improvement requires significant preplanning and time for development of materials and equipment.
(6) Improvement will be composed of several components.

CONSIDERATIONS IN CHOOSING WHAT STRATEGY TO USE

The decision regarding the most appropriate approach to curriculum improvement should be based on the program administrator's logical analysis of the magnitude of the improvement and the immediate and long-term impact of the change. Budgetary implications, the need for staff development, time restrictions, and the availability of appropriate materials and equipment are further considerations that will assist the program administrator in deciding which approach to use. In general, the program administrator should use the most direct method or approach that will ensure an acceptable level of program improvement. The following guidelines may facilitate this decision:

	Improvement	*Magnitude*	*Approach*
(1)	Mandated Change	Minor Import	Authoritarian/ Directive
(2)	Evolutionary Content or Process Change	Minor Import	Curriculum Council Study Group
(3)	Marked Content or Instructional Procedure Change	Major Import	Staff Development/ Inservice
(4)	Improvement Major Curriculum	Major Import	Educational Systems

SUMMARY

This chapter has briefly described current approaches to curriculum improvement: the authoritarian/directive approach, the curriculum council/study group approach, the inservice/staff development approach, and the educational systems approach. Strengths, weaknesses, and applications of these approaches have been presented; and considerations to take into account when choosing what strategy to use have been included.

The demand for quality educational programs requires that the program administrator engage in curriculum evaluation and curriculum improvement. Several curriculum improvement programs may have to be carried on concurrently using a mixture of approaches. Chapter 3 will address the problem of developing the strategy or strategies for curriculum improvement.

3

Developing the Curriculum Improvement Plan

Once an area for curriculum improvement has been selected, a strategy or plan of action must be developed. The administrator as the change leader must devise the steps to "get from here to there." The "here" has been identified during the process of selecting the area for action. This chapter outlines the steps for getting to "there." It provides a broad overview of the role of the administrator in the improvement process and identifies the various components of the process, each of which will be discussed in subsequent chapters.

The administrator must be willing to assume this leadership responsibility, delegating it in varying degrees depending upon the size of the project, the number of staff members involved, resources available, and other local conditions. Under no circumstances can he, or should he, dodge the responsibility for making the final decisions regarding the "what, when, how, how much, and by whom for whom" of instructional changes and improvements. His own support of the project must be active and visible to all if optimum success is to be obtained.

Initially a decision must be reached as to whether the project will be a districtwide, central-office-supervised type of operation or whether it will be carried out with major initiative and implementation in the hands of individual teachers and school staff. Most projects, of course, are a blend of the two, and the decision becomes a matter of degree. Outside consultants, performance contracting, and purchase of specific services should be carefully considered. These decisions should be made during the early stages of planning.

A complete improvement cycle should be developed geared to meet the identified needs of the district or school and to achieve the specific goals of the project. Current literature contains many models and descriptions of the curriculum change and improvement process, ranging from the very simple to the very complex. Some of the better ones are listed in the bibliography.

The plan should contain four major steps, which, while not discrete or mutually exclusive, provide a basic outline for an effective process:

(1) Preliminary planning
(2) Planning for implementation
(3) Initiation and operation
(4) Evaluation and program improvement

Each of these steps serves specific functions and answers specific questions. The preliminary planning phase identifies the project in sufficient detail to:

(1) decide whether it is within the broad goals of the district,
(2) decide whether it is feasible in terms of people, time, and funds, and
(3) obtain tentative approval for its implementation from staff, board of education, professional organization if required, and others concerned with the decision-making process.

The implementation planning phase assumes approval of the project and develops the detail necessary to identify and contract personnel; purchase equipment and supplies; select schools and students to be served; determine costs and allocate funds; set realistic time schedules; and make other management and program decisions.

The initiation and operation phase provides the support and resources necessary to initiate and operate the program and includes continuing support after the initial excitement of "doing something new" has worn off.

The evaluation and program improvement phase is vital to the entire planning process and must provide the decision-makers with the information to intelligently decide whether to continue or drop the program and, more importantly, if continued, what changes should be made if it is to be improved. It is a continuous process and should be provided for during all phases of the program. The entire program should be carefully documented, with all procedures, instructions, guidelines, and explanatory material concisely and carefully written. Reliance on oral or informal communication is very risky and should be avoided. Documentation procedures will vary with the size and type of project; however, two basic written plans are essential. They are a preliminary planning document and an implementation planning document. They may be supplemented with operational memos, supplementary instructions, and status or progress reports, but should never be omitted.

PRELIMINARY PLANNING

Broad guidelines for the project must be established during the preliminary planning period. Questions concerning what you hope to accomplish, how you hope to accomplish it, who will do what for whom, how long it will take, about how much it will cost, who will pay for it, and how you will know how successful you have been must be answered before you move on to detailed planning and implementation. Normally, boards of education and other funding agencies will require answers to these questions before providing support. Proposals for programs requesting Federal funds frequently require the administrator to answer questions of this type and can provide a useful model.

It is essential that this portion of the planning identify the commitment of time, money, personal service, compromise, and active support required of all concerned and that it make the nature and impact of this commitment clear to all. For a teacher to proceed without such a commitment from her principal, the principal without such a commitment from the superintendent or his representative, or the superintendent without a commitment from the board of education, if not sheer folly, is an extremely questionable way to proceed. "Go ahead and try it" is not an adequate commitment; nor is "Try it but I can't allocate any additional funds," nor "Go ahead so long as you don't upset anybody."

Preplanning has three major purposes: (1) to get a firm decision to proceed with the project; (2) to obtain the necessary funding; and (3) to quantify the needed commitment and to obtain it from those responsible for the decision-making process and the allocation of resources. If the preliminary planning document is to serve these purposes it must contain the following information:

(1) Description of the project—who will be served, what will be affected, how and by whom it will be conducted.

(2) Objectives of the program, including measurable changes in student and/or participant behavior.

(3) Review of the literature in the field to provide pyschological support for the project, to identify similar work that has gone on, and to profit from the mistakes and experiences of others.

(4) Delimitation of the problem—student group(s) to be served, number of participants, and content to be covered.

(5) Outline of the proposed steps in the process from preliminary planning to evaluation and program improvement.

(6) Identification of kinds and qualifications of participants, leaders, decision-makers, consultants, teachers, citizens, student representatives, paraprofessionals, resource persons, custodians, etc.

(7) Identification of new positions to be authorized; volunteers to be used, if any; and what services may be contracted with consultants, universities and private organizations.

(8) Orientation, retraining and inservice training needs.

(9) A realistic time schedule and amount of time required for the program. (For projects involving large numbers of schools and/or significant changes in curricular content or method, a minimum of three years is usually necessary. See Chapter 10.)

(10) Role of the community and community agencies, including the identification of resources available outside the school or central office.

(11) The approximate cost of the project (salaries, released time, fees, equipment, supplies, capital outlay, building alterations) and a financing plan and schedule, coordinated with the budget-making process.

(12) Plans for presentation to board of education or other funding agency.

A simplified decision or critical path chart is extremely helpful as a guide to staying on schedule and is a handy checklist to prevent overlooking something.

Consider each item carefully and make a conscious decision on each. Document all key considerations. Do not postpone the facing of an issue or the making of a decision. Have your road map before you start the trip. Use the information gained during the preplanning period to decide whether or not to proceed with actual planning, how large the project will be, and how fast the project will proceed, or whether or not to drop the whole thing.

The decision should take into account local circumstances and resources, and be based upon the following considerations:

(1) Are the needed funds within the resources of the district, or available elsewhere, without robbing programs of equal or more urgent need?
(2) Can people with the needed competencies and experiences be found or trained?
(3) Has the need for the program been clearly established?
(4) Is it compatible with the existing policies and objectives of the district?
(5) Has the research and literature in the field been reviewed and/or have similar programs in other locations been studied?
(6) Are the purposes of the program clearly stated and has provision been made to assess the degree to which the program succeeds?
(7) Are the costs "in line" with the desired outcomes and does the approach appear to be the most economical way to get the job done?
(8) Would the impact of the program have any negative effects upon the existing program? If so, would they offset the value of the new program?
(9) Does the plan provide for testing several ways to achieve the desired results?
(10) Have community and students had part in the planning?
(11) Are most present staff members ready to accept and support the project?
(12) Does the plan really provide the necessary resources to insure a reasonable chance of success?
(13) Can the district provide the management expertise and logistic support necessary, either from existing resources or as a part of the project itself?

(14) Is the time schedule realistic? Does it provide time for review prior to and during budgeting time?

(15) Are there circumstances or conditions in the community that would make the program unacceptable at the time?

Obviously, the administrator must apply professional judgment, in some instances rather subjective, in answering these questions. None the less, if they raise serious doubts in his mind (and/or his staff) he should consider dropping the program, altering it to suit the needs and resources of the district, or postponing it until he has clearer answers to the concerns raised.

For example, in Fairfax County, Virginia, the application of these questions has resulted in the phasing in of certain programs over a period of years rather than "instant implementation." Programs for children with special learning problems, programs utilizing video-tape and other technological advances, the Elementary Science Study program using materials prepared by the school district itself, and the kindergarten and early childhood programs are examples of programs that were implemented only after these questions were considered. This usually resulted in pilot projects, phasing in of the program over a number of years, and extensive in service training and "in-house" preparation of materials.

PLANNING FOR IMPLEMENTATION

Once a decision is reached to proceed with the project, detailed planning for the project must begin and an implementation plan developed. This planning builds upon the preliminary plan and seldom begins at any exact point in the improvement process. The administrator frequently must take a calculated risk, beginning detailed planning prior to budget approval and/or funding. However, at about this point a particular person must be given authority, support, and responsibility for further project development. Planning from this point on can be a part-time job only if the project is a very small one. A superintendent, principal, or other administrator can seldom, if ever, devote the necessary time and energy to the project without neglecting other responsibilities.

At this point the word begins to circulate that "the administration" and "that curriculum study committee" are about to go, or have gone, to the board for approval to begin "that project." Interpretation of the project—its scope, content, and purpose—should be clearly and concisely described and explained to all concerned during this planning-implementation period, and should be repeated at frequent and appropriate intervals.

The main thrust at this time will be the developing of the plan for initiating, implementating, and evaluating the program. This entire process must be carefully documented, covering in detail all aspects of the program and outlining the specific procedures. Objectives of the programs must now become quite specific and quantified in terms of desired changes in performance and behavior.

A single planning, implementation, and operational document should be prepared. Often, limitations of resources, time, experience, and insight will prevent this from happening and a series of memos, materials, and operating instructions may also be necessary. It is essential, however, that the initial implementation planning document includes, as a minimum:

(1) a description of the project,
(2) its philosophy and objectives, and
(3) plans for implementation and operation.

This document should be concisely written, carefully edited, and meticulously reviewed for inconsistencies, ambiguities, and incomplete instructions. It should be completed and distributed as far in advance of the implementation date as possible.

A planning committee, if it is to be used, should have been established prior to or during the early planning stages; the citizen advisory or steering committees should be organized even sooner. The make-up and functioning of committees are discussed in later chapters. The planning committee's duties, responsibilities, and authority must be clearly defined and interpreted to all affected, both those who will gain from the project and those who may feel threatened, with or without cause. Without such definition its authority will be questioned and its work made extremely difficult. Such a group cannot and should not be expected to work out detailed operational instructions and management procedures, nor should it be expected to make final policy decisions. A committee may become a scapegoat because of lack of direction and/or support from the administration or board of education. If it is asked to compensate for the lack of management expertise of the project director or if it becomes, or appears to become, a "rubber stamp" committee, there is little hope that it can function efficiently and effectively.

Description of the Project

The implementation plan should begin with a one paragraph description identifying the name of the project, the population to be served, what will be offered, how and by whom it will be conducted, and what it is hoped to accomplish. This has usually been a part of any preliminary planning document, and with any necessary changes and updating should be taken from this source. If the planner(s) cannot do this in a paragraph of two or three sentences at this point in the project, it probably indicates that further delineation of the project is needed.

Philosophy and Objectives of the Project

Usually any project for curriculum improvement will have both a broad philosophy explaining the reasons for its conduct and specific objectives which it hopes to accomplish. Care must be taken to differentiate between the two as they serve entirely different purposes.

The philosophical reason for a particular project may be drawn from the overall goals of the school district, from the literature in the field, from state and Federal guidelines, or from the work of the planners, planning committees, and project participants themselves. In most cases many, if not all, of these sources may be used. While it is essential that any project have a stated reason for being attempted, care must be taken not to become "bogged down" in writing philosophy, nor should large amounts of time be spent making it razor-sharp at the expense of other parts of the project. It can usually be limited to several paragraphs and expressed in terms of the educational needs of children in general, of children in the district in particular, and the mission of the school district in meeting this need.

In contrast, the objectives at this point must be quite precise, clearly stated, and, in those instances where measurement is intended, must be quantified. Since the objectives will provide the basis for evaluating the success of the project they must be definite enough to serve that purpose. It is no longer acceptable to say that an attempt will be made to improve the reading skills of underachieving fourth grade boys. The objectives should state, "the comprehension level of fourth grade boys who are three or more years below grade level, as measured by test A, will be raised at least two years during the project period."

Objectives should seldom, if ever, be limited merely to academic achievement as just illustrated but should include both the cognitive and affective domains. Attitudes, feelings, appreciations, and values are of equal and, in some cases, greater importance than academic concerns. For example, a unit on Life in Virginia for grades 4-7 developed by the State Department of Education has as its major goal: "To use a concept of role to organize information about different styles of life in rural, suburban and urban Virginia.'"

The objectives under this goal are—

KNOWLEDGE:

- To know that Virginians fill a great number of roles.
- To know that roles are partially determined by location, resources, economics, etc.
- To know some of the roles of the life styles of rural, surburban and urban Virginia.

SKILLS:

- Given information about selected life styles, to identify examples of role.

- Given information about selected life styles, to identify similarities and differences.

ATTITUDES AND VALUES:

- To be interested in finding out more about selected life styles in Virginia.
- To recognize that there are different ways to organize one's life.

Most projects will be effective only if several types of objectives are included.

Fortunately, in the last few years much attention has been devoted to writing educational objectives. Be sure to check your teachers and staff members for this competency before employing outside help. Many graduate courses or portions of such courses are currently devoted to developing educational objectives. Morale will be bolstered by utilizing local staff for such purposes, and lowered if outsiders are used to provide talent available "on board." However, if the necessary skill is not available, universities and other consultants are available.

Examples of objectives written as behavioral statements are:

The pupil sings songs learned in class during free play period.
The student can do twenty push ups in two minutes.
Given fifty multiple choice questions on correct verb usage, the student can answer forty-five correctly.

Current literature abounds with samples of educational objectives written in general or behavioral terms. Several sources are listed in the bibliography. An inservice activity devoted to understanding, interpreting, and preparing objectives can be a valuable part of the pre-operational period.

Operational Procedures

The major portion of the document should be the detailed documentation of the operation procedures for the entire implementation, initiation, operation and evaluation cycle. It is usually not possible to complete it as a single document—a most desirable but difficult aim. If it must evolve as a series of memos, instructions, and committee reports these should be numbered consecutively and disseminated to an established distribution list. Procedural instructions, issued at regular intervals or as needed, may be necessary throughout the first year of the project.

The major procedural areas to be covered, together with an illustrative list with subtopics under each may be grouped as follows:

(1) *Management and Procedures*
   —Calendar for entire cycle.
   —Outline of project, with details on each step.
   —Location of all project activities and meetings.
   —Decision-makers and the decision-making process.
   —Lists of persons and telephone numbers to call for information and support.
   —Responsibilities of support personnel—custodians, transportation, budgeting, purchasing, food services, etc.
   —School and classroom management instructions.

(2) *Program Content*
   —Procedure for determining program content, including program objectives and proposed activities for achieving these objectives.
   —Existing programs and research to be reviewed and utilized.
   —Coordination with existing programs.
   —Criteria for developing, preparing and distributing program and curriculum guides.
   —Instructional methods and procedures.

(3) *Personnel*
   —Identification of numbers and kinds of personnel needed.
   —Job qualifications and job descriptions.
   —Complete plans for inservice training and orientation sessions.
   —Task responsibilities and assignments.
   —Position classifications, salary scales, fringe benefits.
   —Recruiting, interviewing, screening and contracting personnel required.
   —Reassignment of existing staff if appropriate.
   —Utilization of consultants and other contract nonsalaried resources.

—Identification of and guidelines for use of community and parent volunteers.

(4) *Pupils* (or other target population)

—Identification of group to be served—how many, where located, age, sex, socio-economic level, etc.

—Identification of specific individuals by name and location.

—Identification of specific needs of individuals within this group.

—Identification and/or developing of diagnostic and screening instruments as needed.

—Individual diagnosis and screening, if feasible prior to project starting date.

(5) *Facilities, Supplies, and Equipment*

—Identification of all approved supplies and equipment—costs, descriptions, specifications, appropriate use.

—Identification of which options, choices, and substitutions, if any are permissible.

—Procedures for selecting, ordering, and receiving inventory.

—Criteria for selecting and evaluating new materials.

—Building modifications and additional space requirements if needed.

(6) *Financing*

—Establishing costs for personnel, facilities, equipment, materials, and services.

—Preparation of a project budget including all allowable (and nonallowable) expenditures.

—Outline of procedures for expenditure documentation, authorization, and disbursement.

—Options open to the program director and individual program manager to reallocate and reappropriate funds.

(7) *Evaluation and Program Improvement*

—Identification of procedures and instruments for measuring the outcome of the project.

—Procedures and forms for monitoring the progress of the program.

—Outline of the evaluation schedule from beginning of planning through first cycle of operation and program improvement.

—Assignment of responsibility and provision of resources to carry out the research monitoring program.

—Provision to utilize findings to improve the operation and results of the program "on the next go round."

(8) *Communication and Dissemination*
  —Selecting communication devices for dissemination.
  —Incorporating these functions into the planning process.
  —Identification of target groups.
  —Preparation of a communication schedule.
  —Preparation of communiques.
  —Provision for and evaluation of feedback from all target groups.

Since most of these areas are the subjects of later chapters the preceding outline is neither all inclusive nor completely detailed.

It should be emphasized that the implementation plan must be widely received, carefully documented, and disseminated early. Do not decide the day before implementation that the community, school board, students, or chamber of commerce should have participated in the planning. In our present society the privilege of review alone is seldom considered adequate participation. Resist the temptation to say "We don't need to decide on that now, it will work itself out."

INITIATION AND OPERATION

The first few months of any new project are critical. How often the classroom teacher has been given a new book or a new curriculum guide, attended an orientation session, been patted on the back, and left "to go to town!" The administrator must provide extra assistance during the early periods of a new program. He may personally provide leadership or assign it to appropriate individuals and can be most effective by doing both. Frequent (weekly) discussion sessions should be held to review progress or lack of it.

Procedures for communicating problems to those who can assist in their solution must be identified before hand. It must be made crystal-clear that the administration does not expect a trouble-free, smooth running machine from the first day of operation. Problems with busses, lunches, materials, schedules, procedures, pupils, and parents are bound to occur even with the best planning and direction. This fact must be recognized and procedures provided for prompt, if not immediate, remedy. If at all possible, "trouble shooters" should visit the program sites frequently both on a scheduled and a request basis.

Some funds should be held in reserve to meet unanticipated needs. Information should be channeled to the project leader and minor adjustments made as needed. If for no other reason than morale, administrators should visit as many of the project sites as possible. Evaluation and monitoring instruments may have to be changed, funds reallocated, oversights corrected, and commitments reinforced and rededicated.

During the first cycle of operation there must be freedom to vary from the preplanned pattern on operational detail and method without having long delays to wait for administrative approval. The teachers or principal must understand the constraints within which they are expected to operate and must have the support and confidence needed to make day-to-day decisions within these constraints. Distinguish between administrative support and administrative interference. Administrative meddling in the trivia of day-to-day operation can sabotage the entire effort.

EVALUATION AND PROGRAM IMPROVEMENT

Evaluation must not be limited to product evaluation—the assessment of the extent to which the program brought about desired changes in the students or other target populations. It must also include carefully documented process evaluation—the assessment of the effectiveness of the procedures, people, materials, and techniques used. The evaluation must answer two questions: (1) How effective was the program? (2) How can we improve on our performance next time? This section discusses the role of evaluation in the total planning, implementation, and program improvement cycle, providing a general rationale for evaluation and identifying the specific purposes of evaluation. The detailed discussion of evaluation and evaluation procedures is reserved for Chapter 13.

Evaluation must begin with the earliest preplanning activities and extend to the final decision-making concerning whether to continue, modify, or scrap the program. Processes for measuring the extent to which objectives are met should be developed concurrently with the objectives themselves. The evaluation schedule should identify specific points at which certain information will be needed for "go" or "no go" decisions and should include the plan for providing such information. Both the preliminary plan and implementation plan must include the necessary resources—people, time, and funds—to provide the evaluation needed; and evaluation plans should be included as a part of both documents.

However, it is imperative that the objectives of the project and the instruments of evaluation be constantly reviewed to keep the project on course and moving toward the desired target. The teacher (or other participant) must have time for this review, for data gathering, and for documentation. The administrator must see that this time is provided and must insist that this key function be performed. The kinds of data to be collected, the procedure for its collection, and the uses to which it will be put are discussed in Chapter 13.

The need for planning time must be recognized. Allow sufficient released time for those with responsibilities of all kinds and at all levels to get together to discuss mutual problems and concerns, to discuss future plans, to smooth out the operation, and plan for future operation and improvement. Many administrators feel that teachers and teacher organizations are and have been unreasonable and excessive in demands in this area. However, curriculum improvement is at best a slow, tedious, and demanding process. Study the situation carefully. Provide the time necessary to get the job done and see that other staff members, the board of education, and parents understand why such time is critical to the project.

Evaluation should provide an assessment of:

(1) The developmental process used—smoothness of implementation; reception by staff, students and public; pitfalls to be avoided later; savings to be effected.
(2) The effectiveness of the various instructional techniques used.
(3) Value of materials, including written, used.
(4) Need for changes even before end of first cycle.

(5) Need for refinement of the evaluative process itself.
(6) An assessment of the effectiveness of the program in terms of changes in pupil behavior—both cognitive and affective.

This information then provides the basis for improving the efficiency and effectiveness of the program for the next program period.

SUMMARY

Once an area for curriculum improvement has been selected, the administrator should provide the leadership to develop a comprehensive plan for bringing about the improvement. This plan must provide for extensive preplanning, planning and implementation, operation, and evaluation. All persons concerned—students, community, staff, board (including both those who will benefit and those who will feel threatened)—should be involved in all four steps. Duties and responsibilities must be clearly delineated and understood and the decision-making process clearly defined. It is the responsibility of the administrator to make adequate allocations of personnel, time, funds, materials, and equipment. Evaluation must be carefully planned and be going on throughout the process. It must evaluate the procedures and processes used as well as the end product, and provide the basis for dropping, continuing, and/or improving the program.

4

Role of the Key Administrator

The rationale of curriculum improvement, current practices, and a planned strategy for curriculum improvement activities have been described in Chapters 1 through 3. The key administrator, be it the superintendent, instructional supervisor, curriculum specialist, or principal, must assume the responsibility for the direction and management of such activities. This chapter summarizes these responsibilities in broad terms and, in so doing, provides background for the subsequent chapters dealing with specific aspects of the curriculum improvement process.

The management and direction responsibility may be divided into five major developmental steps:

(1) assessing needs and selecting program areas for improvement,
(2) developing the improvement strategy,
(3) managing the project during the implementation phase,
(4) providing for evaluation and program improvement, and
(5) defining and effecting the decision-making process for use throughout the entire project.

The key administrator may perform these functions himself, or assign them to staff members depending on the nature of the project and the size of the school or district. In either case he is responsible for seeing that they are carried out effectively.

He must be identified as enthusiastically supporting the project and resist the temptation to assign blame to others when things are not going well. The project can not be babied or given undue consideration. Responsibilities must be clearly stated, and staff members allowed to assume these responsibilities with authority to carry them out.

ASSESSING NEEDS AND SELECTING PROGRAM AREAS FOR IMPROVEMENT

The key administrator must be the leader in the assessment of the needs of the school or district. This is an expensive and time-consuming process. To assume that it can be done by anyone who has educational experience or be done on a part-time or extra-assignment basis will seriously affect the quality of work done and limit the effectiveness of the project. Assignment to a curriculum improvement activity as a dumping ground for the staff member in trouble or as a "pasture while waiting for retirement" may result in a less than satisfactory needs assessment.

The key administrator must resist pressures and temptations to make such assignments. He must personally initiate and facilitate the assessment of needs and the identification of areas to be improved by:

(1) Clearly establishing that unmet needs are the basis for selecting improvement areas.
(2) Setting up a data base and data collection procedure.
(3) Establishing criteria for selecting programs for improvement efforts.
(4) Providing time, resources, and personnel necessary to do the job adequately.
(5) Setting up an organizational network to ensure the broadest possible participation and the widest dissemination of information.

It is his responsibility to make it quite clear to all concerned that meeting the needs of the school or district is, in all cases, the critical criterion for selecting curriculum improvement areas. He must insist that funds and personnel for improvement be assigned only when the needs have been substantiated. Furthermore, criteria for identifying needs must be established well in advance of assessment. The criteria themselves and the rationale upon which they were developed must be clear to all concerned with the process.

Needs can not be validly assessed unless an adequate base of information is available to the assessor or assessing group. It is the responsibility of the key administrator to make such data available. Much of the data will be already available—some in usable form, some requiring further treatment. The types of data required and possible sources of such data were discussed in Chapter 1. The key administrator must see that data needs are determined and anticipated, that collection and treatment procedures are established, and that the data are available to the needs assessors in time to assist them in intelligent decision making. All too frequently, the data processing system has been finance-oriented and managed by the finance department. Pupil performance information, course data, community characteristics and other information have not been included or have been added as an afterthought. In other instances, the information has been included, but as a separate data system, incompatible with the financial data system, and therefore of limited use. The administrator must remind himself that a single and comprehensive educational information system is essential to all phases of the curriculum improvement process.

All of these activities require people, money, time and expertise which must be well organized and utilized to the fullest extent. The key administrator must provide them and must manage the operation to:

(1) obtain fullest utilization of all resources;
(2) ensure maximum quality and effectiveness of efforts; and
(3) ensure the broadest possible participation and the widest dissemination of information.

 DEVELOPING THE IMPROVEMENT STRATEGY

Curriculum improvement seldom just happens but is the result of a carefully planned procedure and strategy. The overall strategy has been discussed in Chapter 3. As its director, the key administrator is responsible for the entire process. However, there are a number of specific responsibilities to which he should give personal attention and support. These are:

(1) selecting the project director, consultants, and other special personnel;
(2) establishing time schedules and financial restraints;
(3) training and retraining staff members;
(4) interpreting strategy to staff, teachers, board of education and the public;
(5) identifying the decision-making process and assigning such responsibilities;
(6) defining and establishing areas of authority and responsibilities, ensuring that these are maintained and respected;
(7) evaluating the process.

As in all school activities, the key administrator has major responsibility for personnel—the key to the success or failure of the project. He should be actively involved in the decisions concerning the kinds of persons needed; their recruitment and selection; their salaries, benefits and classification; their training or retraining as necessary; the delineation of their authority and responsibility; and the evaluation of their effectiveness.

He must be concerned with the schedule (the critical dates and amounts of time allocated) and must see that it is reasonable and within the limits of effective working procedures and human endurance. He may often have to serve as the buffer between the project workers and difficult and unreasonable demands made by superiors, citizens, boards of education, and others concerned. The task of limiting and establishing the funds available for the project are his responsibility. He has an obligation to all concerned to maintain financial support at a level which will provide the resources necessary for project success. Where adjustments are required, the program may sometimes have to be "cut back." He must ensure that optimum use is made of all funds but must, at the same time, not attempt a program without adequate financial support.

The establishing of who will make what decisions, when, and by what procedures must not be left to chance. Well conceived, potentially effective improvement projects have often been buried in the decision-making process. The decision-makers (board of education, superintendent, faculty, or whoever) must be identified; must be informed of their responsibility; and given the information, time, and authority needed to make the decisions. The decision-making schedule must be correlated with the budget-making process, with the school schedule, and other established school activities. Criteria for decision-making should be carefully developed.

Evaluation and decision-making are closely related and the key administrator must see that they are complementary. Interpretation and dissemination of the program must be as carefully planned as any part of the program. These activities are covered in detail in other chapters.

PROGRAM MANAGEMENT
DURING THE IMPLEMENTATION PHASE

The key administrator must recognize that even with the best personnel, all necessary resources, and the best strategy for operation, success is not guaranteed. It is imperative that the project be continually monitored and assessed. To the extent possible, he must see that the project stays on schedule, that it does not stray too far from its original objectives unless by intent, and that problems and frictions are quickly identified and corrected.

He must be responsive to the changing needs, anticipate difficulties which the project may encounter, and develop a flexible project management system which allows: the reassigning of authority and responsibility; the reallocation of resources (time, people, material, money); and the prompt communication of project progress, difficulties and new decisions to all concerned. This prompt, direct communication, both internal and external, is critical to project success but will not take place accidently.

Even with the best plans, some "head-knocking" will usually be necessary. Some personnel will prove unsuited for the new assignment, some not selected will feel resentful, and some who feel their status is threatened will resist the project, either passively or by verbal sabotage. These problems should not be overlooked but should be dealt with promptly and forthrightly, and as positively as possible.

Once initiated the project must be nourished, nurtured, and protected. This is a responsibility that the key administrator must assume—one he must not dodge or delegate to a subordinate.

EVALUATION AND PROGRAM IMPROVEMENT

Evaluation is of little or no value unless it results in the expansion, curtailment, discontinuance, or improvement of a regular or pilot program. Except in the very small school or school district, the key administrator will probably not perform the actual evaluation. His major responsibilities are to ensure that:

(1) objectives and evaluative techniques have been developed in advance of implementation;
(2) evaluation, dissemination, and program continuation are part of the funding and allocation procedures;
(3) an audience of decision-makers review the findings and make a commitment that subsequent action will be based thereon.

He must see that evaluation procedures become the basic process by which curriculum improvements are effected and that they become a part of the established operating policies of the school district, complete with the necessary funding, personnel, district, and school understanding, and a commitment to support.

DEFINING AND EFFECTING THE DECISION-MAKING PROCESS

A clearly defined decision-making procedure is essential if the project is to move ahead smoothly and on schedule. The key administrator must:

(1) hammer out the decision-making process in advance;
(2) set a decision-making schedule, complete with check points;
(3) define the school board's role in the decision-making process;

(4) assume responsibility for providing the input necessary to inform the decision-makers;

(5) plan the decision-making process so that it is coordinated with the budgeting and funding process.

The importance of clearly defined decision-making procedures is emphasized throughout this book. It is one of the most important responsibilities that the key administrator must assume if he is to be an effective leader of the curriculum improvement team. Once the process is established and made a part of the operating policy, it must be carefully followed.

THE KEY ADMINISTRATOR IN ACTION: A CASE STUDY

An illustration of the role of the key administrator in directing and managing curriculum improvement activities can be provided by the activities of the director of a regional educational development center.

Operating over a three-year period under a Federal grant, this center was responsible to an executive board composed of district superintendents. The center was responsible to:

(1) assist with comprehensive studies of educational program, needs, and resources, and

(2) assist administrators in local school districts individually and regionally in determining and developing specific project and program proposals.

The director, as key administrator of the education development center, employed a program development and research staff, and worked with the executive board to determine a rationale and framework for the initiation and implementation of programs.

A preliminary survey of school programs and supplementary services existing in the 240 elementary and secondary schools of the seven-county region was undertaken during the project's initial year in order to assess the status of existing programs and services, and to determine priority educational needs. A summary of survey results indicated as priority needs (in rank order) the following programs and services at the elementary level:

(1) Reading specialists
(2) Guidance services and specialists
(3) Special Education programs ✓
(4) Physical Education programs
(5) Psychological Services; Library Services; and Early Childhood Education
(6) Health Services; Teacher Aide Programs
(7) Instructional Materials Services; Educational Television ✓
(8) Training of Substitute Teachers
(9) Music Education; Training of Teacher Aides
(10) Art Education; School-Community Cultural Resources

Follow-up surveys included a study of existing private kindergarten and preschool programs, a study of critical teacher shortages, and a study of the incidence of children with exceptional educational needs. These research, evaluation, and survey activities were carried out in order to identify areas of immediate and long-term regional needs.

Data from the needs assessment activities were presented to the regional executive board to assist the board in reaching decisions relative to areas for program improvement. Over the next two and one-half years, the regional center developed and implemented the following programs at the direction of its executive board:

(1) A seminar and exemplary school site visitation program for superintendents and school board members.
(2) A staff development program for potential school principals.
(3) A preservice and inservice program for teachers and administrators on the development and utilization of instructional materials and educational technology.
(4) An experimental third-year general mathematics curriculum with built-in staff development activities for new teachers.
(5) A demonstration project for preschool mentally retarded children with built-in opportunities for teacher training and certification.
(6) A program designed to assist a school district desegregate its schools.
(7) A demonstration kindergarten and nursery school program.
(8) A program designed to train and certify teachers in areas of critical needs.

In addition to these projects, continuing seminars and "interest conferences" were held to provide inservice experiences for educational personnel in areas of priority need. The guiding principle in the development and implementation of programs and services was that emphasis would be given to activities that would be regional in scope and impact.

The pertinence of this illustration rests in the fact that the director of the regional center was responsible for developing and implementing programs that (a) were based on identified priority needs, (b) met with the approval of an executive board, (c) required the employment of staff, (d) required continual program management during program operation, and (e) required continued communication with the decision-making body during the operation of programs.

SUMMARY

This chapter has presented an overview of the role of the key administrator in the curriculum improvement process. The major roles discussed included assessing needs and selecting program areas for improvement, developing the improvement strategy, managing the project during the implementation phase, providing for evaluation and program improvement, and defining and effecting the decision-making process for use throughout the entire project. In Chapter 5, we will deal with organizing and staffing for curriculum improvement.

5

Organizing and Staffing for Curriculum Improvement

Personnel of the right kind and in appropriate numbers is the key to curriculum improvement, whether it be through a special improvement task force group or whether it be accomplished with existing school or curriculum staff organizations. The individuals working with the curriculum improvement program must be blended together as a team; they must be carefully selected, fairly paid, and classified in relation to existing staff. The kinds and numbers of personnel needed must be determined based upon identified tasks to be performed.

This chapter discusses these and related matters in the following sections:

(1) Determining the kinds and numbers of personnel needed.
(2) Evaluating present utilization of staff.
(3) Using district personnel vs. recruitment and employment from outside.
(4) Recruiting, screening, and selecting personnel.
(5) Protecting rights and status of existing staff members.

DETERMINING THE KINDS AND NUMBERS OF PERSONNEL NEEDED

The first step in organizing and staffing for curriculum improvement is the determination of the kinds and numbers of personnel needed. Needs must be established based upon an analysis of jobs to be done, which have been determined based upon the objectives of the curriculum improvement program. The competencies required should be carefully identified, quantified, and described since they will be used during recruitment, selection, salary determination and classification, inservice training, and evaluation.

Attention should be directed toward all personnel service requirements ranging from direction and supervision to clerical and custodial. Many of these services will, can, and should be provided by existing instructional and support staff. In other instances, personnel will have to be employed from outside the system or made available by reassignment from within the school staff. The district budget and staff requirements provide documents as a means of checking to see if essential services will be provided, since the improvement project will usually need most of the services required for the regular program. Professional personnel needs for a large school district are illustrated in Figure 5-1 by a job group listing from the Fairfax County, Virginia, Public Schools. Similar listings are usually available within school districts for technical and supporting services personnel.

FAIRFAX COUNTY PUBLIC SCHOOLS

SALARY JOB GROUPS

Job Group I
  Media Coordinator
  Research Technician
  Science Helping Teacher
  Staff Library Specialist

Job Group II
  Food Service Supervisor
  Media Specialist

Job Group III
  Media Design Specialists
  Coordinator of Head Start Programs
  Director, Neighborhood Youth Corps
  Elementary Assistant Principal
  Intermediate Guidance Director
  Personnel Assistant

Figure 5-1

Supervisor of Teacher Training, ESS

Job Group IV

Area Subject Specialist
Assistant Supervisor of Audiovisual Services
Assistant Supervisor—Special Education
Athletic Director and Director of Student Activities
Coordinator of Step-Up Language Arts
Intermediate Assistant Principal
Library Services Assistant Supervisor
Planning Analyst
Psychologist
Secondary Guidance Director
Assistant Supervisor for Manpower Training
Intermediate Assistant Principal

Job Group V

Area Coordinator of Pupil Services
Elementary Principal (to 17 Teachers)
Instructional Specialist
Project Director, ESS
Subschool Principal
Secondary Assistant Principal
Apprenticeship Coordinator
Assistant Supervisor—Adult Services
Coordinator of Grant Programs
Educational Technologist
Personnel Specialist

Job Group VI

Evening Principal
Elementary Principal (18-39 Teachers)
Food Service Director
Program Research Specialist
Research Specialist

Job Group VII

Coordinator of Year-Round School Study
Curriculum Specialist
Elementary Principal (40-59 Teachers)
Intermediate Principal (40-59 Teachers)
Library Services Supervisor

Figure 5-1 (Continued)

Personnel Coordinator—Educational Personnel
Personnel Coordinator—Support Services
Personnel Supervisor—Compensation
Personnel Supervisor—Employee Relations
Secondary Assistant Principal for Administrative Services
Supervisor of Audiovisual Services
Supervisor of Special Education

Job Group VIII

Director of Adult Services
Assistant to the Division Superintendent
Associate Principal
Coordinator of Media Services
Coordinator of Pupil Services
Coordinator of Research and Testing Services
Coordinator of Vocational Education
Director, Center for Effecting Educational Change
Intermediate Principal (60-99 Teachers)
Personnel Supervisor—Staff Development
Secondary Principal (60-99 Teachers)

Job Group IX

Area Administrator
Coordinator of Curriculum
Personnel Supervisor—Selection

Job Group X

Director of Personnel
Secondary Principal (over 100 Teachers)

Figure 5-1 (Continued)

The following guidelines will prove helpful in determining the kinds and numbers of personnel needed:

(1) Allow more staff for a pilot or beginning program than is customary for an existing operational one. This is necessary because of the unique needs of such a project which include planning, documentation, developing of objectives and goals, evaluation, communications, and inevitable mistakes and false starts. However, avoid creating the impression that the improvement group is special—overstaffed, over-supported, and overpaid.

(2) Don't overclassify. Resist the tendency to "go after" a given person

regardless of the cost. Classification of curriculum improvement personnel at an obviously higher level than existing staff may doom the project to failure.

(3) Provide adequate support personnel including clerical, custodial, technical, and other personnel as needed. Don't neutralize the potential effectiveness of the professional staff by making it necessary for them to perform routine support functions.

(4) Design the program, then select the staff. Don't create "spots" for certain persons.

(5) Determine staff needed based upon specific program requirements. Information such as the following is essential:

- Target population—numbers, characteristics, geographical location
- Number of schools to be served
- Financial constraints and procedures
- Job classifications and pay scales
- Amount of special training that will be needed
- Amount of evaluation expected
- Duration of the project
- Facilities and equipment required and available

(6) Consult and visit functioning programs in other districts.

(7) Base needs upon a proposed organization and administrative plan. While an organizational chart never tells the entire story, it should precede and serve as the basis for identifying the kinds and numbers of personnel needed. Resist the temptation to always put a person in each organizational box. Except in very large projects, several functions can usually be performed by one person.

EVALUATING PRESENT UTILIZATION OF STAFF

The administrator does not have unlimited funds. In fact, he must frequently show improvement without additional resources or must use present resources in the curriculum improvement program. Better use of existing personnel is frequently demanded before additional support is made available.

By far, the most expensive resources are people. Up to 80 percent of the budget may go for salaries. The following questions will assist the key administrator in determining whether or not the existing staff members are being utilized effectively and effi-

ciently, and can provide the basis for reassignment and reallocation of personnel within the district.

(1) Does a job description exist for each position? Does each employee
know the limits of his job?
(2) Are employees evaluated in terms of the specific objectives established for their jobs?
(3) Are positions created for some who have not been successful at
previous assignments?
(4) Is there a program for on-the-job improvement of skills and competencies?
(5) Do supervisors, curriculum specialists, program analysts, and re-
searchers have the means to ensure that their work becomes input
for decision-making?
(6) Do we have "overtrained" personnel; e.g., a principal with a masters
degree and twenty years experience supervising custodians?
(7) Does the district utilize the latest information processing techniques
and office technology?
(8) Is clerical and technical support adequate, or are professional persons
providing their own services?
(9) Are power struggles and personality clashes blunting the improvement
thrust?
(10) Are certain critical skills and professions missing on the district staff?
(11) Does everyone have at least some knowledge of what's going on?
(12) Are your top change leaders free to lead, or are they tied down with
details and administrative arrangements?

The answers to these questions should provide the administrator
with an indication of how well present staff is being utilized.

USE OF DISTRICT PERSONNEL VS.
OUTSIDE RECRUITMENT

Curriculum improvement programs may be staffed by reassignment and retraining of existing personnel, by employing new
personnel from outside the district, or a combination of the two.
A mix of existing staff members and newly employed personnel is
desirable. The following considerations will prove helpful in the
personnel selection process:

(1) Screen existing staff carefully—don't unintentionally bring in a less qualified outsider and have to admit overlooking a highly qualified person within the district.

(2) If a project requires new talents not currently being used in the district, don't assume that they are not available within the existing staff. It is difficult, if not impossible, to know the competencies that staff members have brought to your district. It is embarassing, wasteful, and morale-lowering to have to say, "Gosh, Mary, if we had known you had that background, we would have used you."

(3) Don't assign marginal or unsatisfactory producers on the current staff to the curriculum improvement team, "just to have a place for him" or "where he can do the least damage." On the other hand, view such projects as an opportunity to give a staff member a change of pace, an opportunity to grow, an opportunity to prepare for broader responsibility, or a chance to expand his professional expertise.

(4) Don't strip existing programs of their strength and expertise. This will cause the improvement program to be suspect from the beginning, and weaken already functioning programs.

(5) Often, promising staff members and teachers can be trained with reasonable or minimum effort. It frequently provides professional growth for the staff, both those being trained and those doing the training. Consider this alternative to outside recruiting very carefully.

(6) Take into account the existing teacher supply and demand situation and the decreasing enrollment trend as they affect your district. Don't overload with new staff in the face of imminent cutbacks.

(7) Provide for temporary assignments to the curriculum improvement project. Allow existing staff an opportunity to participate with the option of returning to the regular instructional setting.

RECRUITING, SCREENING AND SELECTING STAFF

The key administrator must assume personal responsibility for personnel management. In larger school systems, he should assign his most competent personnel officer to the task. All the rules and guidelines for personnel management should be applied with great care and skill when staffing for curriculum improvement. The task is extremely difficult because:

— competencies and people new to the district may be required,

- responsibilities and operational procedures are not firmly established,
- the administrator may not have had experience in the fields to be covered,
- the feelings, rights, and professional pride of present staff must be protected,
- personal characteristics may be more crucial than professional experience and training,
- to a greater degree than usual, the selection must involve some guesswork, some "playing of hunches."

The personnel manager must take these considerations into account when recruiting, screening and selecting the curriculum improvement staff.

Recruiting

Recruiting activities may be quite limited or very extensive, depending upon the size and nature of the project and the availability of the kinds and numbers of personnel needed. The following guidelines will prove useful in the recruitment process:

(1) Advertise all positions—perhaps even more extensively and enthusiastically than regular vacancies.
(2) Recruit systematically, both inside and outside the school system, and within the limits of any negotiated agreements with professional organizations. However, don't overlook personal contacts and recommendations of associates.
(3) Recruit armed with all the necessary facts, such as a job description, a description of the project, a candid assessment of the "pros and cons" of the assignment, an indication of its duration and job security, salary schedules and fringe benefits, opportunities for professional growth and advancement, working conditions, and rules and regulations of the district.
(4) Don't oversell during the recruitment process; an oversold applicant is likely to become a disgruntled employee.
(5) Recruit through as many avenues as possible; e.g., the media, colleges and universities, existing files of present employees and applicants, directors of similar projects, employment agencies, state departments of education, and other governmental agencies.

(6) Consider employment of professionals from other fields for technical, management, and support functions.

Screening and Selecting Applicants

The screening and selecting process is a continuation of the recruiting process leading to the actual employment of staff. Procedures should be based upon the same considerations outlined for recruiting. In addition, there are a number of other considerations:

(1) Screen from the list of available applicants a limited number for serious consideration based upon the identified background, experience and expertise needed for the position.
(2) Use a committee for final screening and selecting of personnel from this list for all management, supervisory, and professional positions.
(3) Have all the information discussed in the preceding section available during the screening and selection process. If a committee is used, furnish this information plus qualifications and experience of all candidates to committee members well in advance of interviews.
(4) Include in the interviewing process the proposed method for evaluating the applicant's performance, once employed.
(5) Be frank about the job—the uncertainties, the headaches, the biases of the staff, and the frustrations that may be a part of the job. Curriculum improvement is seldom the appropriate area for the faint of heart.
(6) Be prompt in notifying those applicants not selected, particularly if they are members of the existing staff. Don't let them get "the word" via the grapevine.

PROTECTING THE RIGHTS AND STATUS OF
EXISTING STAFF MEMBERS

Preceding sections of this chapter have focused on the need for recognizing existing staff during the staffing process and will not be repeated here. Several additional considerations are pertinent, however.

(1) Explain, explain, and explain the entire project to existing staff; keep the entire project in the open.
(2) Explain the recruitment, screening, and selecting process to existing staff, and explain why more staff may be needed for the project than currently operating programs.
(3) Include regular staff on all planning, personnel selection, and implementation committees; have particular concern for those who may feel that their status and future is threatened by the project.
(4) Orient the project staff to the importance of good relations with the existing staff. Pushy, officious, and demanding curriculum improvement teams can wreck the most carefully planned curriculum improvement projects.

The key administrator must continually monitor the program to see that the good human relationships necessary to the effective conduct of a curriculum improvement project are maintained and improved throughout the program. He cannot ignore his responsibility to both the curriculum improvement team and the existing staff throughout the entire process.

ILLUSTRATIVE ORGANIZATION FOR CEEC

The Center for Effecting Educational Change (CEEC) was an on-the-job attempt of the Fairfax County Public Schools to develop a systematic procedure for bringing about desired educational improvement in a large suburban school district. It was a Federally funded project unter Title III of the Elementary and Secondary Education Act.

As stated in the grant application, its purpose was:

To develop and initiate a systematic change procedure for bringing needed improvements in the public and non-public schools in Fairfax County, Virginia and to utilize this procedure for implementing changes in selected areas of the instructional program.

Figure 5-2 shows the organization and the personnel employed to bring about these objectives. Because of major emphasis on

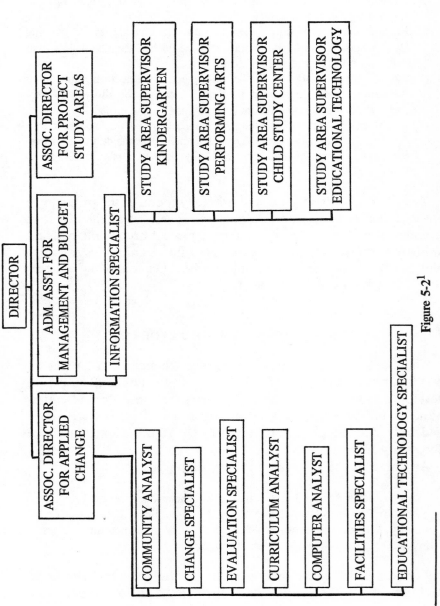

Figure 5-2[1]

[1] Reproduced from *The Operation of a Center for Effecting Educational Change*, Fairfax County, Virginia.

research and nationwide dissemination, the number of positions in the Applied Change section is larger than would normally be required in any but the largest school districts.

This organizational structure is included, not as a model to duplicate, but to show the various competencies required to effect curriculum improvement, utilizing the systematic approach discussed throughout this book. The study area supervisors are not permanently assigned, but are selected to work in the curriculum area(s) under study at any given time—in this case kindergarten, performing arts, a child study center, and educational technology. Districts should develop their own organizations and establish their own personnel requirements, combining several of these functions in a single position, eliminating those not needed, perhaps providing some of the functions with existing staff, and making other adjustments to meet local conditions and needs.

Several of the job descriptions used are reproduced here to illustrate how such descriptions might be written and to show, in greater detail, the responsibilities, work assignments, and qualifications for selected positions. (See Figures 5-3, 5-4, 5-5 and 5-6).

The Center for Effecting Educational Change has been continued with local funds, once the Federal grant expired, and is currently being absorbed into the regular structure of the school district's research, planning, and evaluation arm. Many of the lessons learned from its successes, partial successes, and failures (and there were quite a few of the latter) are reflected throughout this book.

1. *Position Title*

   Associate Director for Applied Change

2. *Duties*

   The Associate Director for Applied Change will be responsible to the Director for:
   — Developing the philosophy, purposes, and procedures for the operation of the Center
   — Directing the Applied Change staff
   — Conducting research and study of educational change
   — Developing a staff approach to assist Study Area Educational

Figure 5-3

Teams and providing other services as needed by Study Area Supervisors
— Supervising the Applied Change Center staff in providing other services to the staff members of public and nonpublic schools
— Assisting in the preparation of staff professional papers and regular information bulletins and dissemination of all information about the Center to public and nonpublic school personnel and the total community and utilization of the existing school media services through the office of School-Community Relations
— Performing other duties as are appropriate to the attainment of the objectives of the Center

3. *Qualifications*

Personal qualifications to include:
— Advanced degree, preferably a doctorate, in educational research, psychology, or related fields
— A minimum of five years' experience in education, including teaching, supervision and/or administration with practical experience in several of the following fields:

Research and survey
Community planning and coordination
Program development and implementation
Systems analysis or data processing
Curriculum development and evaluation
Development of educational specifications for schools or other education types of facilities
— Skill in writing or experience as an editor supervising writing and publication of documents similar to those required for the dissemination of Center information
— Deep personal interest in improving education through the application of Systematic Change Procedure.

Figure 5-3[2] (Continued)

---

[2]Reproduced from *The Operation of A Center for Effecting Educational Change,* Fairfax County, Virginia.

1. *Position(s) Title(s)*

    Study Area Supervisors for:
    Kindergarten
    Child Study Centers
    Educational Technology
    The Performing Arts

2. *Duties*

    The Study Area Supervisors will be responsible to the Associate Director for Project Study Areas for:
    - Utilizing the total resources of the Center and the on-board staff to direct the planning and the conduct of pilot studies in Selected Project Areas
    - Determining the content of pilot programs
    - Acquiring or developing curriculum guides and other instructional materials
    - Identifying personnel needs in terms of competencies and numbers and assisting in the selection of personnel
    - Identifying children to participate in pilot studies
    - Developing and conducting training and retraining of staff
    - Supervising classroom activities
    - Working with the Center staff and the on-board Department of Research and Program Development staff in developing evaluative instruments and criteria
    - Working with the Educational Technology Specialist in determining the extent to which educational technology may support the pilot program and to effect the appropriate application
    - Determining alternate approaches to be tested along with pilot projects
    - Assisting the on-board staff with the many details of implementation (the year following the conduct of the basic pilot program) of the program, follow-up of the program, and evaluation of the program
    - Maintaining coordination between the on-board staff and the Center staff during all phases of the program
    - Maintaining close working relationships with the nonpublic school officials to ensure that that service—either direct service to pupils or indirect service in the form of inservice training or the development of the materials—is extended

Figure 5-4

to the nonpublic school students and teachers on a basis consistent with the total service to be provided to an identified population
— Performing other duties as appropriate to the attainment of objectives

3. *Qualifications*

Academic, Experience, and Personal qualifications to include:
— Minimum of master's degree in a field appropriate to the Project Study Area
— Minimum of three years' successful experience in administration and/or supervision preceded by successful classroom teaching or other appropriate experience
— Demonstrated ability in research, curriculum development, and evaluation (or other appropriate areas)
— Personal qualities indicating success in working as a team member in applying total team resources to the solution of problems.

Figure 5-4[3] (Continued)

1. *Position Title*

Community Analyst

2. *Duties*

The Community Analyst will be responsible to the Associate Director for Applied Change for assessing the general attitudes toward change in Fairfax County by:
— Serving as a member of the Applied Change Staff and Study Area Educational Teams, performing the following tasks:
— Conducting in-depth analyses of needs and resources in selected Project Study Areas with particular emphasis on the assessment of the causes and effects of change on the total educational and cultural program on the public and nonpublic schools and the various nonschool educational and cultural agencies
— Assisting with the identification of the needs and characteristics of the pupils to be served, including analysis of anticipated initial behavior

Figure 5-5

---

[3]Reproduced from *The Operation of a Center for Effecting Educational Change,* Fairfax County, Virginia.

- Identifying community forces affecting children and developing procedures using these forces positively
- Conducting comprehensive research and surveys of needs and resources in Fairfax County
- Providing technical assistance to teachers and other staff members in the public and nonpublic schools
- Assisting with dissemination activities of the Center, including the preparation of articles and other materials describing the change process and the function of the Center
- Performing other duties as are appropriate to the attainment of the objectives of the Center

3. *Qualifications*

Academic, Experience, and Personal qualifications to include:
- Bachelor's degree plus graduate work (preferably a graduate degree) in education, sociology, public administration or related areas
- Successful work experience in community analysis, preferably in a field other than education
- Ability to work objectively with community groups
- A personal interest in directing community forces toward the improvement of education.

Figure 5-5[4] (Continued)

1. *Position Title*

Change Specialist

2. *Duties*

The Change Specialist will be responsible to the Associate Director of Applied Change for:
- Serving as a member of the Applied Change Staff and Study Area Educational Teams, performing the following tasks
  - Working as a team member with the Center staff, particularly the Curriculum Analyst, to devise a Systematic Change Procedure
  - Working with the Community Specialist and the Information Specialist when needed in creating the proper climate for, and positive attitude toward, change

Figure 5-6

---

[4]Reproduced from *The Operation of A Center for Effecting Educational Change,* Fairfax, County, Virginia.

     — Working closely with the Evaluation Specialist in determining the immediate effects of change and the probable long-range effects, and implementing alternate courses of action when appropriate

     — Collecting and interpreting the research on change process in general and in selected Project Study Areas

     — Conducting research about the change process in selecting Project Study Areas with emphasis on the causes and effects of change and the implications to the educational and cultural programs in Fairfax County

     — Assisting with the implementation of the Systematic Change Procedure over on to three-year periods

     — Coordinating the change process within the Center and within the total resources of the community, keeping in mind the effect that change may have on the existing total program

     — Analyzing on a continuous basis the forces affecting change, including the resistance to change, in the various Project Study Areas

     — Providing technical assistance to teachers and other staff members in the public and nonpublic schools

     — Assisting with dissemination activities of the Center, including the preparation of articles and other materials describing the change process and the function of the Center

     — Performing other duties as are appropriate to the attainment of the objectives of the Center

3. *Qualifications*

Academic, Experience, and Personal qualifications to include:

     — Master's degree in social psychology, anthropology, sociology, behavioral sciences, or a similar field

     — Three to five years' experience in interpreting and predicting change in certain areas

     — Sincere personal ambition to avoid stereotyped approaches through creative action.

Figure 5-6[5] (Continued)

---

[5]Reproduced from *The Operation of a Center for Effecting Educational Change,* Fairfax County, Virginia.

6

The School Staff - Key
to Improvement

The need for curriculum change and improvement must be of continuing concern to the administrator. For many years, schools and the people who run them have been under attack for their alleged lethargic approaches to curriculum change. This may have been true in the past, but today, change is occurring at an ever increasing rate and is being generated from a new source, the individual school staff.

This chapter will deal with the involvement of the school staff in the curriculum improvement process with major emphasis placed on:

(1) Staff involvement in curriculum improvement
(2) Levels of planning for curriculum improvement
(3) Determining what needs improving
(4) Developing goals
(5) Developing work plans
(6) Determining acceptable levels of improvement

STAFF INVOLVEMENT IN CURRICULUM IMPROVEMENT

Traditionally, changes in schools and school curricula have resulted from external forces and pressures. Curriculum specialists determined what the school needed, and it then became the administrator's responsibility to implement the change necessary to meet these needs. Today, many of the important changes and improvements are resulting from efforts of educators working on the "inside" who are experiencing the need for improvement on a first-hand basis.

The atmosphere in the school community has changed. No longer will the school principal and his staff accept change, or lack of it, solely on the basis of mandate or tradition. Each component of the curriculum is being examined in terms of relevance. The emerging specialist is in the classroom of the local school and is examining the curriculum in terms of its appropriateness to his particular situation. The idea that curriculum can be developed in isolation, and students fitted to it, is disappearing rapidly.

The curriculum of today must meet the needs and requirements of students who are in a particular school or classroom at a particular time. Broad, general, comprehensive plans must be made at the district level, but if the curriculum is to be current and vibrant, guidelines must be established that will not only allow adjustment and change to take place at the school level, but will encourage it and allow it to take place rapidly as the need occurs.

It is not intended or recommended that the key administrator relax all constraint and allow helter-skelter, trial and error adjustment in the curriculum. It is suggested, however, that a plan be developed that will require each staff member to examine his particular area of responsibility and make adjustments and improvements in order that the program better serve the needs of students.

The plan presented here is not intended to represent a one-shot curriculum improvement effort. Once implemented, it becomes a continuing, recurring and integral part of the total school improvement program requiring that each staff member:

(1) selects an area or areas in his own personal sphere of responsibility that needs improvement,
(2) makes specific plans for assuring that the improvement occurs, and
(3) evaluates the results.

Freedom of action and involvement of staff in the curriculum improvement process are the keys to success. The right of the individual to select areas of personal concern for improvement produces a high degree of positive commitment, thus improving expectations for success. Involvement is achieved by requiring each staff member to examine his program and develop specific plans for improvement. In order to accomplish this in an orderly manner, each staff member must state specifically what he intends to accomplish in terms of goals. When the plan has been in operation for a time, the administrator will discover that much of the negative attitude regarding change disappears. Change occurs constantly and no longer presents a threat. When the plan has been fully implemented and accepted by the staff, change, regardless of magnitude, is handled routinely and efficiently. Before improvement goals are discussed in detail, there must be a discussion of the levels at which goals are produced and the relationships of goals developed at one level to goals developed at another.

LEVELS OF PLANNING FOR CURRICULUM IMPROVEMENT

As discussed earlier, this is not a helter-skelter procedure, but one that allows considerable freedom within broad general constraints in order that there be freedom and direction simultaneously. Goals must be identified at the district, school, departmental, and classroom levels with the degree of specificity established. Success of the plan is dependent on commitment at each level. The plan presented below assumes involvement of an entire school district. This plan is only a model—levels may be added or deleted as required to meet local needs.

(1) *District Goals.* Goals developed at this level should be broad and general in nature with major emphasis directed toward systemwide improvement. The list of objectives developed should be adequate to cover major areas of concern, but not so comprehensive as to be overwhelming.

(2) *School Goals.* Goals developed at this level should be somewhat more specific than those stated at the district level. They should reflect the intent of district level goals, but they should deal with areas of concern at the local school level.

(3) *Departmental or Grade Level Goals.* Goals developed at this level should be developed jointly by members of departments or teams of teachers. They should be specific and should further the intent of district and school goals.

(4) *Individual Teacher Goals.* The goals at this level are developed by the individual staff member and represent identification of problems the staff member wishes to address personally. These goals should be specific in nature and relate to those developed at other levels.

Illustrative district, school, departmental and/or grade level, and individual teacher goals are presented later in this chapter.

If a plan such as this is to be adopted on a districtwide basis, district goals must be formulated as a take-off point. The person with this responsibility must prepare, publish and distribute these goals along with other literature explaining the plan. In preparing the goals, care must be exercised to ensure that each statement is that of a goal to be achieved, as opposed to the description of an activity. Examples of goals and objectives will be presented later in this chapter.

DETERMINING WHAT NEEDS IMPROVING

When district goals have been formulated and before staff members can be expected to begin preparation of individual, departmental, or school goals, the principal must be certain that each member of the staff has a clear understanding of the plan and of his specific role within it. Simply stated, the plan is intended to involve staff members at each level in the improvement of the curriculum and/or the school or school system. Each individual has the responsibility for identifying areas that need improvement, developing improvement goals, preparing improvement strategies, determining acceptable levels of improvement, executing this plan, and evaluating the results. Before beginning work on the plan, each staff member must ask himself the following questions:

(1) What specific problems or pupil needs do I encounter continually that need attention?
(2) What, specifically, can I do to improve these conditions?
(3) How will I determine the degree of improvement?
(4) What will represent acceptable levels of improvement?

When these questions have been answered satisfactorily, the individual is ready to begin preparation of his improvement goals.

Role of the Principal

Direct involvement in curriculum improvement may be a new experience for many staff members. The administration is assigning primary responsibility to each person, and is asking each to bring concerns into the open and focus on them. Approached properly, this will be a very positive experience. Few teachers have been allowed or expected to make specific, original documented contributions to curriculum improvement which are based on personally identified needs. This new experience may appear threatening unless the staff has been properly prepared. The principal must provide benevolent protective support. He must act as the resource person who provides the stability and direction to members of the staff as they work their way through a new and taxing experience. Guidance, encouragement, and understanding are his key responsibilities at this time.

The success or failure of the plan must not be associated with teacher evaluation. Creative approaches to curriculum improvement are being sought. The teacher is being asked to identify specific areas of concern and develop plans to improve them. Improvement is sought, but it is quite possible that a teacher may identify an area of concern, develop goals and improvement plans, carry them out, and still find that the situation has not improved. Teacher concern about possible failure of a curriculum improvement plan should be kept at a minimum. If fear of failure pervades, the plan may degenerate into an exercise where teachers select improvement areas in which they feel secure and certain of success. Each success and failure must be viewed as a learning experience that provides information valuable for future use.

DEVELOPING GOALS

District Goals

If this plan is to be implemented on a divisionwide basis, the first step is the development of district goals. These are usually developed by the superintendent and/or his staff. Involvement of principals, teachers, and other members of the staff will encourage commitment to district goals. When the district goals have been formulated, they, along with instructions and explanatory material, must be published and distributed in order that each staff member is aware of the plan and his responsibility in the execution of it.

Examples of district level goals are as follows:

(1) To ensure that each student attains and maintains proficiency in basic academic skills.
(2) To ensure that each student masters the basic knowledge and research skills necessary to a life of continuing education.
(3) To ensure that each segment of the community is afforded maximum opportunity to participate in the development of the district's programs.
(4) To ensure improved school—community relationships.
(5) To ensure maximum return from financial resources expended.

School Goals

After district goals have been formulated, the action moves to the school where schoolwide, departmental, and individual goals must be developed. There is no specific order for their development; however, they should be closely related and interdependent. Usually, they are developed concurrently, requiring conferences, consultations, meetings, and discussions. Occasionally, there are confrontations.

It is at this point that the principal plays his most important role. He must disseminate and interpret the district goals, explain them, develop a calendar, provide work time, establish deadlines, and delineate requirements and responsibilities. He must plan, organize, initiate, adjust, reorganize and, in essence, orchestrate, until all goals are finalized. There is no "cookbook" procedure that will produce desired results and the planning and execution must be left to the principal.

Examples of school level goals are as follows:

(1) To ensure that each student attains and maintains proficiency in the basic mathematics skills.
(2) To ensure that each student attains and maintains proficiency in basic language arts skills.
(3) To ensure that each student attains and maintains grade-level proficiency in reading skills.
(4) To provide improved community participation in program development.
(5) To provide improved communication between the school and the community.
(6) To provide improved student safety through better auto-traffic control.

While it is expected that all staff members will support all of the district goals, the individual should be concerned only with those specific goals that will receive personal major emphasis during the year. In the preceding school level examples, goals 1, 2, and 3 relate to the first district goal. Goal 4 above relates to the third district goal. Goal 5 relates to the fourth district goal; while goal 6 above does not relate to any of the district goals but represents an area of major concern to the principal and his staff.

It is assumed that each staff member will support all goals developed at a higher level, but he is not required to respond specifically to each goal developed at the higher level, nor is he limited by them. Each individual is free to develop goals that are pertinent to his individual situation.

Departmental and/or Grade Level Goals

Goals developed for this example are for the seventh grade mathematics department in the school and district for which the preceding goals were developed.

To ensure that each seventh grade student masters the basic manipulations of addition, subtraction, multiplication and division of whole numbers, fractions, decimals and percentages.

In this particular case, the department chose to state only one goal which relates to a specific district and school goal.

Individual Teacher Goals

These example goals were developed by a seventh grade mathematics teacher in the department for which the departmental goal above was developed:

(1) To ensure that each student masters the basic manipulations of addition, subtraction, multiplication and division of whole numbers, decimals, fractions and percentages.
(2) To ensure that each student masters the multiplication tables, 1 through 12.
(3) To ensure that each student retains the skills mastered.

DEVELOPING WORK PLANS

After each staff member has identified goals for the coming year, he must establish the procedure to be followed to attain each goal. This procedure is called the work plan and must be specific. A work plan should be prepared for each goal.

For example, the mathematics teacher stated as one goal that she would ensure that each student in seventh grade mathematics would master the basic manipulations of addition, subtraction, multiplication, and division of whole numbers, decimals, fractions, and percentages. Her work plan for this goal might be as follows:

(1) *The Stanford Diagnostic Arithmetic Test—Level II, Form W* will be administered to each entering seventh grade student.
(2) On the basis of the results of this test, a profile of strengths and weaknesses will be charted for each student.
(3) Based on this student profile, individualized instruction will be planned for each student.

(4) Other forms of the standardized test will be administered at the end of each grading period.

(5) The individual profile will be updated and, based on the profile, individualized instruction will be planned for the student each time the test is administered.

(6) The final updated mathematics profile will become a part of the student's permanent record to be utilized as a starting point for the following year.

DETERMINING ACCEPTABLE LEVEL OF IMPROVEMENT

Once a goal has been determined and work plans prepared for attaining it, the person preparing the goal must then make a decision as to what will constitute an acceptable level of improvement. On first effort, the stated performance levels may miss the mark widely because they may have been set too high or too low. With experience and refinement, it becomes relatively easy to establish realistic performance levels for improvement. As with work plans, acceptable levels of improvement must be developed for each goal.

The math teacher who identified mastery of the basic manipulations as a goal may wish to state performance levels for improvement at the end of the year as:

(1) Ninety percent of all seventh grade students will demonstrate mastery of the basic manipulations of addition, subtraction, multiplication, and division of whole numbers, fractions, decimals, and percentages as evidenced by the standardized test.

(2) All students will have improved by at least five percentile points in mastery of these basic skills as measured by standardized tests.

CALENDAR AND ILLUSTRATIVE FORMS

When the decision is made to commit a school district to a project such as this, a calendar must be prepared to insure coordination and continuity. Obviously, a plan as far reaching and all-inclusive has budgetary implications; therefore, where possible, the school improvement calendar should coordinate with the calendar developed for budget preparation. Procedures should be established for review and evaluation of individual, departmental, school, and district curriculum improvement efforts in terms of achievement of desired goals. The results of this evaluation and review should result in modifications as the program improvement procedure begins a new cycle. With this in mind, the school improvement calendar should be planned in such a way as to ensure that all plans for the coming year are complete before the end of the current year. Time must be provided in order that each individual may have adequate time to plan, prepare goals and work plans, and to review authority. Before the end of the school year, each staff member must have his plan complete in every detail and ready for implementation when the new school year begins.

Seen as a total package, this plan may appear cumbersome and difficult. Broken out into its components, it becomes a realistic plan for curriculum improvement and results in commitment and enthusiasm on the part of the staff. With this plan in effect, the school staff becomes the major force in curriculum improvement.

In order to ensure uniformity and organization, forms should be prepared for staff members to use as they work on their improvement plans. See Figures 6-1, 6-2, and 6-3 for sample forms with illustrative entries.

School Improvement Plan

Location: A Junior High School

Goal:

> Level II: 1. To ensure that each student maintains proficiency in basic mathematics skills.

Work Plans:

> 1. *The Stanford Diagnostic Arithmetic Test–Level II, Form W* will be administered to each entering student.
>
> 2. A skills profile will be developed for each student.
>
> 3. On the basis of this profile, individualized instruction will be planned for each student.
>
> 4. A different form of the test will be administered at the end

Figure 6-1

of each grading period and the profile will be updated and instruction adjusted.

Acceptable Level of Improvement

1. All students will demonstrate maintained proficiency in basic mathematics skills.

2. On the basis of the standardized test, 95% of the students will improve at least five percentile points in mastery of identified basic mathematic skills.

Reviewed by: The Principal

Review Date: _____

Figure 6-1 (Continued)

Departmental Improvement Plan

Location: A Junior High School

Department: Mathematics (7)

Department Chairman: Miss Smith

Goal:

Level III: To ensure that each 7th grade student masters the basic manipulations of addition, subtraction, multiplication, and division of whole numbers, decimals, fractions, and percentages.

Work Plans:

1. *The Stanford Diagnostic Arithmetic Test–Level II, Form W* will be administered to each entering student.

2. A skills profile will be developed for each student.

3. On the basis of this profile, individualized instruction will be planned for each student.

4. A different form of the test will be administered at the end of each grading period and the profile will be updated and instruction adjusted.

Figure 6-2

Acceptable Level of Improvement

1. All students will demonstrate maintained proficiency in basic mathematics skills.

2. On the basis of the standardized test, 95% of the students will improve at least five percentile points in mastery of identified basic mathematic skills.

Reviewed by: The Principal

Review Date: ―――――――――

Figure 6-2 (Continued)

Individual Improvement Plan

Location: A Junior High School

Department: Mathematics

Teacher: Miss Jones

Goal:

Level IV: To ensure that each student masters the multiplication tables 1 through 12.

Work Plans:

1. Administer diagnostic test to determine mastery of this area.

2. Develop mastery profile for each student.

3. Plan individualized programs for each student.

4. Administer similar test at end of each grading period and update profile and adjust instruction accordingly.

Acceptable Level of Improvement

1. All students will demonstrate improved mastery of this area.

2. 85% of the students will attain the stated goal.

Reviewed by: The Principal

Review Date: ―――――――――

Figure 6-3

7

Communicating During the Improvement Process

Communicating about education is one of the greatest problems facing the educator today. In an era of rising costs and increasing taxes, the competition for public support becomes sharper every year.

Also, the competition for public attention gets keener as time goes on. More leisure time and more money to spend during it; technology which has provided more communication opportunity through television; and increased competition from government agencies, as well as commercial enterprises, have all increased the difficulty in having a message used and in getting people to listen to it. While a collection of press clippings is gratifying to the "clipper," their value is whether anybody really listened to them.

It is only natural that support of public education, which consumes considerably more than half of the budgeted expenditures in most local jurisdictions, should be a prime target for budget reduction. This is further complicated by criticism of public education and the tendency to place the blame for most social ills on education and educators: e.g., drug problems, antigovernment activities, or lack of discipline. The list seems almost endless, and the fiscal conservative, particularly the activist who has no children in school, makes liberal use of the list.

A particular target of criticism is the educational innovation— the year-round school, the open classroom, team teaching—and

95

not without some justification. Too often such innovations have been instituted without adequate preparation of staff, parents, and students, and this has often doomed them to failure from the start.

Communication about curriculum improvements must start early, be continuous, and be thorough. Also it must be regarded as the job of everybody—the administrator, the principal, the teacher. Too often we find the educator leaving this job to the professional communicator.

This chapter will be devoted to some of the techniques that the key administrator should use in planning and executing the communications program:

(1) Planning and timing.
(2) Identifying target groups.
(3) Choosing the communications vehicle.
(4) Preparing the message.
(5) Evaluating the communications program.

PLANNING AND TIMING

The success or failure of any curriculum improvement depends upon the caliber of planning done prior to initiation, and during and after implementation. The communications plan should be an integral part of the overall design of a curriculum improvement project.

Who is to do this planning? If a professional communications staff is available to work with the curriculum planners, it should be a part of the planning team from the outset. Professional communicators in the community should not be overlooked as resources, nor should teachers or administrators who either have training or have evinced an interest in communications. A small system may find the volunteer communicator the best source of help in this area.

Timing should be considered carefully. It is a vital part of communications. Many educational innovations have never gotten under way because communications about them have been too little or too late. Scheduling is vitally important.

IDENTIFYING TARGET GROUPS

One of the first steps in planning for communications is the identification of the various groups to whom the message will be directed. A brief discussion of some of the more important of these groups, designated as target groups, is presented below.

Internal Groups

All groups that comprise the school district staff (e.g., teachers, administrators, support personnel, custodians, clerical personnel), students, and the board of education are considered internal groups for the purposes of communication.

These are the first and most important groups toward which communication must be aimed. Without their support from the beginning, all may be lost. It must be recognized that many people by their very nature are not amenable to change and feel threatened by any innovation affecting their way of life. Communication with these groups must be constant and comprehensive to be successful (the death of many innovations has occurred before they really had much of a chance to live because of misunderstanding, hostility, resistance, and even sabotage by internal groups). Communications with them must run the entire gamut from inservice programs, briefings, and observation of innovational programs to written communications such as newsletters and fact sheets. These internal groups include:

Teachers and administrators. The real key to success is the support and understanding of teachers and administrators. These groups are usually most affected by the introduction of innovation since an innovation may change their working life (or they may feel it will). It may require a great deal of effort on their part to implement and it may require changing work habits and teaching methods that are satisfying to them. In any event, failure to gain their support and understanding will reduce the chances for program success significantly.

Other employees. Too often in education, there is a tendency to overlook or disregard support employees. This is unwise as they also constitute an important internal public which wants to be part of the "family." Support personnel frequently play a key role in introducing innovation; for example, calendar changes such as year-round school have a considerable impact on support functions (maintenance, transportation, custodial, food services, supply), and the understanding and support of personnel performing these functions are vital.

Students: Educators have frequently overlooked the most important group of all—the students—in developing understanding of a curriculum improvement. It is extremely important to communicate with all student groups, particularly those at the secondary level. They are increasingly activist and vocal, and should be carefully considered in the communication program. Their leaders should be included in planning and in all phases of communication. Students have considerable influence on parental attitudes toward education and education innovation, and can be very effective in communicating about them.

Boards of Education. Boards of education and other governing bodies which control education and educational financing are obviously highly important. Their support is essential for they control educational policy, and even more importantly, its financing. They must be thoroughly briefed on the innovation and must be supportive of it. The degree of support is of particular importance and must be strong enough to withstand pressure from opposing parents and pressure groups. Communication with them must be early, continuous, and effective for the innovation to succeed.

External Groups

While it is sometimes difficult to separate external groups from internal groups, the more important external groups include:

Parents of students. The more important parent groups such as parent volunteers, PTA leaders, and citizen advisory committees will be the opinion leaders of the parent public. The most effective communications device is a happy, successful, learning child. However, the great majority of parents are apathetic until something occurs to threaten their children or which they feel may have an adverse effect on them. Then they can become "tigers." While communication should be aimed at all parents, don't overlook the importance of the opinion leaders.

Pressure groups. Pressure groups are usually composed of parents, some with a general interest in education, such as the PTA, and others promoting a special interest: e.g., special education, compensatory education, music. Most civic groups are generally supportive of education although there are some that oppose paying the cost of education. They usually tab the educational innovation as a "useless frill," and their support is difficult, if not impossible, to obtain. However, having the understanding and support of the pressure groups is essential to success. Very few governing boards and senior administrators can withstand the "heat" generated from the many pressure groups who may oppose a particular innovation. If their support is gained, they can be highly instrumental in success and they should be a prime target of communications.

General public. The general public includes singles, childless couples, and older persons whose children have completed school. While some of these constitute the "anti-education" pressure groups, the majority are usually apathetic. Educational innovations are the favorite target of the conservative "antis." "Innovations or program improvements are unnecessary frills and another step toward the 'ruin' of our educational system." They are a difficult and elusive target to reach; however, they cannot be ignored as a communications target.

CHOOSING THE COMMUNICATIONS VEHICLE

A coordinated communications plan must be developed if there is to be effective communication with all the identified target groups. No channel or vehicle should be overlooked. They should all be included in a coordinated communications plan. Some of those which have proved most effective, together with ways of using them, are:

Face-to-Face

The most effective means of communication is "face-to-face," and should be used whenever possible. Among the opportunities are:

(1) Inservice programs for teachers and administrators—PTA, student leaders, and other community leaders supportive of education should also be included.
(2) Speakers' bureaus with well-prepared speakers offered to PTA and civic organizations.

(3) Briefings for student leaders including student government and advisory council groups.

(4) Briefings for opinion leaders including heads of key organizations. These can be the most important catalyst of community opinion to help get public acceptance.

(5) Parent briefings, open houses, coffees, and luncheons at the local school level.

Mass Media

News releases, pictures, feature suggestions, and illustrated articles should be planned for release to the media. All the media should be included in planning. Following are some suggestions:

(1) *Radio and Television.* Periodic studies show that more and more people are getting the majority of their news from these sources, and they should be emphasized. Among the effective uses of the media are:
   — Preparation and distribution of specially tailored releases for use by radio and television should be included. They will be used particularly by small radio stations which do not have the staff capability of rewriting standard news releases into their format.
   — Feature materials emphasizing human interest aspects offer opportunities for the brief coverage given by radio and television.
   — Taping of programs and messages—even the brief question/answer type—will find ready acceptance by radio stations, which have a Federal requirement to provide air time as a community service.
   — Closed circuit television, if available, should be included as a valuable tool for briefing staff, students and parents.
   — CATV (when it has its own telecasting facility) and educational television should be included in plans as valuable media outlets, not only for feature material, but also for panel and discussion types of programs.

(2) *Newspapers.* Many of us have the tendency to think of the value of newspapers primarily in terms of feature material in metropolitan dailies. Of course these are important, and planning for communications about curriculum change should include getting the metropolitan dailies involved in the communication program. However, don't overlook the following:
   — Suburban and rural dailies and weeklies depend on and thrive on local news. They sometimes operate on a shoestring with small staffs

and eagerly accept well-written news releases and feature articles with pictures. They can be a bonanza in the acceptance of outside material and pictures as contrasted with large papers, which are usually hampered by union rules and pride from using other than staff-written material.

— The advertising and throw-away paper is similarly anxious to accept well-prepared educational material to fill the spaces between advertisements and to make the paper more appealing.

— The freelance writer in the community should be considered a good vehicle for getting feature material into dailies, weeklies, and educational publications. Free lancing is a big business on a part-time and full-time basis. Many talented people are so engaged and are naturally hungry for story material and help.

Miscellaneous Vehicles

Among the miscellaneous vehicles that can be used are the following:

— Newsletter from the central administration level and the local school level (from principal and PTA) are extremely valuable tools for communicating to both internal (employees) and external (parents) groups. Plans should include provision of material for these. They need not be fancy publications to be effective, nor does the material need to be elaborate. Some of the most effective are mimeographed or dittoed on a single sheet. Inclusion of a series of questions and answers can be highly profitable.

— Brochures and fact sheets for the public may be distributed; and newsletters for parents may be mailed, distributed through the schools at PTA meetings, or carried home by students. Where a mailing list is maintained at the central administration level and/or at the individual school level, newsletters and other material should be provided to those on the list, who are usually the opinion leaders in educational matters.

— A call telephone on which messages of various types can be recorded offers an inexpensive and effective tool. It can serve a dual purpose: as a phone for the media to call for information (and from which a message may be recorded for use on radio), and as a "hot line" for staff and public. Again, a series of questions and answers can allay many concerns as they arise or, better yet, before they arise.

— Information centers or phones can be established for answering questions and discussing concerns. Their being manned by parent volunteers further enhances public support.

Fairfax County Information Vehicles

The Fairfax County information program includes a wide variety of publications, brochures, and news releases which are used to inform the public, staff, and parents on school matters and which devote significant space to curriculum and curriculum improvement matters. Among the more effective are:

(a) *A monthly Bulletin*—a printed slick paper publication complete with illustrations, articles from teachers and staff members and comments by the superintendent which goes to staff members and other selected persons. Each issue is devoted to a discussion of a school program, either instructional or support. Curriculum areas and improvements covered in the last eighteen months included health, art instruction, math, music, physical education, special learning disabilities, and the use of volunteers in the school. The *Bulletin* is usually sixteen pages long and is not included here.

(b) *Supergram*—a weekly newsletter to all employees and others on the mailing list. 16,000 are printed weekly. While this publication covers administrative and general interest items, it also includes summaries of curriculum studies and instructional programs. Note the item on year-round education and Interschool (Figure 7-1).

(c) *Agenda of School Board Meetings*—the agenda is published one week prior to Board meetings and is sent to staff, schools, interested citizens, and leaders of community groups. Notice the three items related to curriculum improvement on the sample copy included as Figure 7-2. The recipients of the agenda then receive a summary of the board meeting which is published the day after the Board meeting is held. This summary includes Board discussion and any actions taken.

(d) *Familygram*—a newsletter for parents published twice yearly. Included as Figure 7-3.

(e) *Condensed news releases* for radio and television. These are in addition to regular news releases and stories (Figure 7-4).

(f) *Informational brochures* published on various school subjects and programs. The three included here as Figures 7-5, 7-6 and 7-7, deal with general information, kindergarten, and the standardized testing programs.

FAIRFAX COUNTY PUBLIC SCHOOLS

SUPERGRAM

from the DIVISION SUPERINTENDENT
10700 PAGE AVENUE
FAIRFAX, VIRGINIA
Editorial Offices · 691 2291

No. 135   September 25, 19__

FCPS HAS 117 NATIONAL MERIT SEMIFINALISTS

A tip of the SUPERGRAM hat goes to the 117 Fairfax County high school seniors who have been named National Merit Scholarship semifinalists. All 20 Fairfax County high schools which have senior classes are represented. The semifinalists are among 15,000 named nationwide and will compete for some 3,100 merit scholarships to be awarded next spring.

MODEL UN SET FOR NOV. 12-14

The annual Fairfax Model United Nations Program (FAMUN) will be held at Hayfield Secondary on Nov. 12, 13, and 14. The coordinator for the program is Rod Clemmons, Hayfield.

SUPERGRAM CALENDAR

Sept. 27 - Employee-Management Relations Committee 1:30 p.m., Board Room

RADIO REPORT CARD HITS THE PLAYING FIELD ●

The girls' varsity field hockey team from Stuart High will be this week's guests. The Groveton High Band will provide the backup music. Airtimes:

Saturday, Sept. 29
11:00 a.m. -- WOHN (1440 AM)
Sunday, Sept. 30
7:45 a.m. -- WEZR (106.7 FM)
8:30 a.m. -- WPIK (730 AM)
11:00 a.m. -- WOHN (1440 AM)
8:30 p.m. -- WEAM (1390 AM)

DO YOU WANT RADIO PUBLICITY?

As part of its weekly broadcast, Radio Report Card will announce upcoming school events that are open to the public. If you would like your school's particular activity cited in the "School Calendar" segment of the program, please submit your request to Lynda Forsythe, School-Community Relations, 691-2291, two weeks prior to the actual event. We will try to work in the notices as time permits.

FIRST 'ARITHMETIC PROJECT' SHOW

On Monday, Oct. 1, at 2 p.m., the first part of Lower and Upper Brackets, a film from "Arithmetic Project," will be shown on WNVT-53. The second part will be shown on Thursday, Oct. 4, at 3 p.m. The film is one of those to be used during the course which will begin Nov. 1 (details in Aug. 21 SUPERGRAM). During the first week of each remaining month of the school year another film from the Project will be shown at the same time (Mondays at 2 p.m. and Thursdays at 3 p.m.) with repeats on Tuesday mornings at 8 a.m.

RED CROSS ENROLLMENT DRIVE

Superintendent Davis has approved the Red Cross enrollment program for the 1973-74 school year. Principals will be contacted shortly by Mrs. Jane H. Dickerson of the Fairfax County Chapter of the Red Cross.

YEAR-ROUND STUDY TO CONTINUE ●

Following study of the year-round education report and recommendations which had been received from the staff at the Sept. 6 meeting, the School Board last Thursday directed the staff to continue planning for potential implementation of a pilot study starting in July 1975. The Board action included the following:

...The pilot study would be conducted in one high school community--a high school and its feeder intermediate and elementary schools.

...The objective of the test would be to study educational benefits and improved space utilization.

...The staff was directed to recommend more than one high school community for intensive communications dialogue about year-round education. Before the communities are selected, the Board will require an outline from the staff on the scope and content of the communications program.

...The staff was further directed to improve and expand the cost analysis of a pilot test and to concentrate on a study of the job opportunity situation at the high school level in a year-round program.

...Finally, the Board committed itself to holding a countywide public hearing on year-round education before a final decision is made on implementation of a pilot study.

SICK LEAVE BANKS' ENROLLMENT PERIOD

Eligible employees are reminded that they have until Oct. 1 to enroll in the appropriate sick leave bank if they have not already done so. For bus drivers, the enrollment period this year will be extended through Oct. 31. For information or to obtain enrollment forms, call Miss Donna Crack, 691-3263.

SALUTE TO FCPS BUS DRIVERS

A tip of the SUPERGRAM hat goes to FCPS' 648 dedicated and competent bus drivers who drove more than 4,400 student runs on Friday, Sept. 14, under the most adverse weather conditions without an accident. Many of the drivers are new this year and had less than ten days of pupil transportation experience when the torrential rains hit.

FCPS TO GRADUATE 79 ADULTS

Superintendent Davis will be the speaker at the graduation ceremony for 79 people who have completed high school in the adult high school program. The commencement is Sept. 27, 8 p.m., at Annandale High.

VEHICLE WASH FACILITIES AT TWO SITES

The School Board has awarded a contract for construction of automatic vehicle wash facilities at the Newington and Jermantown maintenance sites. To be used jointly for county and School Board vehicles the facilities will be jointly funded by the Board of Supervisors and the School Board.

Figure 7-1

Louise Foster, language teacher at Frost Intermediate, participated recently in a workshop at American University. This was an orientation meeting with the Fulbright-Hays foreign exchange teachers. She worked with the language teachers.

ENERGY CRISIS TIP

Remember that in most vehicles, and under most traffic conditions, it is rarely necessary to depress the accelerator more than a quarter of the way to the floor. Any more will waste fuel and cause extra wear to tires, engines and transmissions.

PHONE
DIRECTORY
CHANGES

The number has been changed for the following schools: Fort Hunt High to 360-5800, Woodson High to 323-1911, and Frost Intermediate to 323-1317.

DIRECTIVES ISSUED IN AUGUST

Not. 1300	8/27	– American Education Week
Reg. 1511.2	8/1	– Music Instrument Dealer Participation in School Demonstration Programs
Not. 1619	8/21	– Schedule of Courier Service
Not. 2003	8/31	– Commitment to Education (PPBES)
Pol. 2361 (Amendment)	8/2	– Students
Not. 2381	8/21	– Membership Reports, Elementary, Intermediate, and High Schools
Pol. 2491	7/31	– Religion in the Schools
Reg. 2491	7/31	– Religion in the Schools
Not. 3420	8/20	– Monthly Financial Report to Program Managers (July)
Not. 3610	8/14	– Student Accident Insurance 1973-74
Not. 4150	8/1	– Assignment and Transfer - Special Teachers 1973-74
Not. 4431	8/17	– Salary Supplements
Reg. 4431.3	8/17	– Salary Supplements
Not. 4440	8/17	– Local Supplemental Retirement System for Educational Employees (central administration staff only)
Not. 4510	8/14	– Special Education--Inservice Calendar, 1973-74 School Year
Reg. 5351.3	8/21	– Purchase and Installation of Air Conditioning Units with Local Funds
Not. 5530	8/23	– Mobile Supply Service Unit (MSSU)
Reg. 5550	7/19	– Accidents
Reg. 5560	7/30	– Weather and Emergency Conditions--Precautions
Reg. 5950	8/23	– Accident Reporting Requirements
Not. 6110	8/22	– Film Booking Procedures
Not. 6217	8/13	– Elementary Education - Social Studies (elementary schools only)
Not. 6217	8/13	– Intermediate Education - Social Studies (intermediate schools only)
Not. 6217	8/13	– High School Education - Social Studies (high schools only)
Not. 6301	8/10	– Instructional--Countywide Meetings
Not. 6510	9/30	– General Educational Development Program - Schedule of Testing
Not. 6616	8/10	– Standardized Tests and Testing

Call 691-2446 for missing directives.

*Account Clerk I S-8 (11 months)
   Kilmer Intermediate

Custodian III (field custodian) A-4-2
   Area II
   Area III

Carpenter Helpers (2) A-4-2
   Structural Maintenance

Refrigeration Equipment Repair Helper A-4-2
   Mechanical Maintenance

Electric Motor Maintenance Helper A-4-2
   Mechanical Maintenance

Custodian II A-3-2 (based on seniority)
   Fairfax Elementary
   Floris Elementary (Herndon)
   Hunters Woods (Reston)

Bus Driver Aides S-2-1
   Transportation Department

Applicants for positions with asterisk should apply to Supporting Services Personnel (691-2483). All others should complete an Application for Promotion or Transfer form to be received by the Supporting Services Personnel Office (691-2481) no later than Wednesday, Oct. 3, 4:30 p.m.

TUITION REIMBURSEMENT

Employees requesting tuition reimbursement must provide with the form evidence of satisfactory completion of the course. Requests from educational employees will be retained until the end of the fiscal year, at which time funds available will be divided prorata among all those requests approved. Only one three-semester-hour course per employee per year will be reimbursed. If there are questions call Miss Donna Crack, 691-3263.

'INTERSCHOOL' ON WNVT

"Interschool," a new WNVT-53 program, during the week of Oct. 1-5 will take a look at a brainstorming session on use of television programs in lesson plans. Specific suggestions and a process of television usage in lesson plan development will be suggested. Airings will be on Monday at 8:30 a.m. and 3:30 p.m., Tuesday at 3 p.m., and Wednesday at 8 a.m. Questions? Call Melodee Rosen at WNVT, 323-7000.

TEXTBOOK RECEIVING, ACCEPTANCE PAPERS NEEDED

Schools that have received textbooks directly from publishers must return the receiving and acceptance reports immediately, as these purchases are on a 30-day net payment basis. Send the reports to Textbooks Section, Material Requirements Division, so that payments can be made to publishers by the end of the month.

STUDENT RECORDS, ONE FROM GERMANY

Cumulative records for Garth Lasater, forwarded from Germany, are being held at Rolling Valley Elementary. If this student is registered at your school, please call Rolling Valley, 451-7410. Missing are the records for Chris Cowden, between Holmes Intermediate and Annandale High. Chris records should be forwarded to Annandale.

SOCIAL STUDIES MEETING CHANGED

The date for the first meeting of the Social Studies Curriculum Committee has been changed from Sept. 26 to Oct. 3, 3 p.m., at Lake Braddock, Division of Curriculum Services.

Figure 7-1 (Continued)

agenda
date of meeting
at

FAIRFAX COUNTY SCHOOL BOARD
FOR FURTHER INFORMATION, CALL 691-2291

November 8, 19__, 8:30 p.m.
(Executive Session, 8 p.m.)

School Administration Building, 10700 Page Avenue, Fairfax, Virginia

8th Meeting - Regular

8:30		Meeting called to order by presiding chairman	
8:31		Roll Call	
8:32	I.	Adoption of the Agenda This agenda is adopted with any recommended changes approved by the Board.	ACTION
8:34	II.	Approval of Minutes Minutes of the October 23, 1973, Board meeting are submitted for approval. These have been prepared by the Clerk and distributed to Board members in advance for review.	ACTION
8:35	III.	Business Affairs The records of petty cash disbursements for the month of September are presented for Board review and approval.	ACTION
8:37	IV.	Transportation Recommendation to reprogram $160,000 from FY 1974 funds for the purchase of 23 special education buses for FY 1975.	ACTION
8:50	V.	Special Education A. Proposal for a federal grant to provide staff development for teachers of learning-disabled children. Under the program, 30 teachers would be trained each semester, working in a school with 240 children with learning disabilities.	ACTION
		B. Status report of the Division of Special Education to include staffing and program development.	INFORMATION
		C. Authorization for additional staff for special education.	ACTION
9:30	VI.	Pilot Program Recommendation on a pilot study at Freedom Hill Elementary School for a career education model, grades K-6, which has been approved for state aid.	ACTION
9:45	VII.	Construction Confirmation of Board action at November 1 work session re contract award for heating, ventilating, and air conditioning for Caldwell and Dogwood Elementary Schools.	ACTION
9:50	VIII.	Environmental Quality Advisory Council/School Board Joint Effort Staff response to recommendations from EQAC Educational Committee concerning environmental educational programs in the school system.	INFORMATION
10:20	IX.	Superintendent's Reports The Superintendent presents items not listed separately for Board consideration.	
10:30	X.	Board Matters Each Board member is given an opportunity to introduce subjects for consideration.	
10:45	XI.	Adjournment	

Delegations or individuals desiring to receive information on agenda items or to address the Board are advised to communicate with the office of the Division Superintendent.

ACTION AND INFORMATION items are so noted after each listing on the agenda

Figure 7-2

Fairfax County Public Schools

FAMILYGRAM

Published twice each year for citizens of Fairfax County

S. John Davis, Division Superintendent • Sept. 19__ • 10700 Page Ave., Fairfax, Va. 22030

Dear Parents:

This is the first issue of FAMILYGRAM, a publication for parents of Fairfax County Public Schools students.

Communicating with all the publics in a school system as large as ours is a difficult task and, at times, one of the most frustrating we face. Despite all of our efforts, I know that communicating with each parent from the county level needs much improvement.

I hope that FAMILYGRAM will help in this regard. We expect to publish twice this year--now and at the start of the second semester--to give you news about your school system.

We want your reaction to this publication to include material you would like to see incorporated in future issues. Write me, or call in your suggestions--to 691-2291.

We are looking forward to this school year with a determination to do a better job than ever before in providing your children with an outstanding education. I am confident that you will, as always, give us your help and support.

S. John Davis

S. John Davis
Division Superintendent

DID YOU KNOW THAT?

...Fairfax County, the nation's 15th largest school system, has about 136,000 students attending 168 schools.
...More than 6,000 classroom teachers are employed to teach your children.
...One of the nation's largest school bus fleets, consisting of more than 640 buses, delivers over 83,000 students from home to school and back home again each school day.
...It takes about 1,100 food service employees to serve about 65,000 hot lunches each school day.
...The school system has an operating budget of about $155.2 million this year.
...It will cost an average of $1,154 to educate each student in the system this year. This ranges from a low of $752 for each elementary student to a high of $3,567 for each youngster in special education.
...Of last year's 9,200 high school graduates 73 percent are going on to higher education this fall with about 56 percent attending four-year colleges and universities.

FIRST SEMESTER CALENDAR

Sept.		
	4	First day of school
	10	Fall adult classes begin
Oct.		
	1	Superintendent's Forum, Areas I and II--Jefferson High, 8 p.m.
	8	Columbus Day holiday
	10	Superintendent's Forum, Areas III and IV--Robinson Secondary, 8 p.m.
	21-27	American Education Week--plan to visit your children's schools. Also see student art exhibits and demonstrations at Tysons Corner and Springfield Mall
	22	Veterans Day holiday
	27	Fairfax County Public Schools on Parade--Springfield area
Nov.		
	8, 9	Student holidays
	22, 23	Thanksgiving holidays
Dec.		
	24	Winter holidays begin
Jan.		
	2	Students return to school
	25	First semester ends
	28	Student holiday
	29	Second semester begins

COME TO THE SUPERINTENDENT'S FORUM

As noted in the calendar, Superintendent Davis will hold two forums in early October. Organizations and individuals are urged to attend and make comments and recommendations on the FY 1975 budget. Following the budget discussion, parents will be invited to ask questions on any school subject. This will be an opportunity for parents to meet with Dr. Davis and members of his staff on an informal basis. School Board members are also expected to attend.

BROCHURES TO KEEP YOU INFORMED

A series of brochures is being published about various aspects of Fairfax County Public Schools that should be of particular interest to parents. Available now at the nearest school or area office:

...Welcome to Fairfax County Public Schools
...How the Area Organization Can Serve You
...Kindergarten--The First Step

Soon to come are brochures on Standardized Test Scores for 1972-73, Community Use of Schools, and others.

Figure 7-3

THREE SECONDARY SCHOOL BUILDINGS OPEN

As school opens this fall three new secondary school buildings are being occupied.

...Chantilly, located on Stringfellow Road, just off Route 50 adjoining the west boundary of the Greenbriar subdivision, is a 2,500-pupil building. Opening initially with students in grades 7-10, it is expected to become a high school (grades 9-12) when a projected intermediate school is built nearby. Chantilly's principal, Dr. Robert S. Davis, formerly principal of McLean High, has been on the job for more than a year preparing for opening of the new school.

...Lake Braddock, located on Burke Lake Road near the Kings Park Shopping Center, is Fairfax County's third 3,900-student capacity secondary school (the others are Hayfield and Robinson). It also opened with students in grades 7-10, and like Chantilly, its principal, John W. Alwood, formerly principal of Edison High, was assigned to this post more than a year ago.

...The third facility, Mount Vernon High, houses the students from one of Fairfax County's oldest high schools. The 2,800-pupil building has been constructed at the site of and includes the former Whitman Intermediate building. Whitman Intermediate in turn opened this fall in the old Mount Vernon building on Route 1. Mount Vernon has a new principal also--Thomas J. Hyer, who has replaced retired principal Melvin B. Landes.

Finally, on the secondary level, Woodson High School reopened this fall in its building on Route 236. The Woodson building suffered about $1 million damage in a tornado last April which necessitated Principal Robert E. Phipps, his teachers and students, moving to Oakton High for the remainder of the school year. Repair of the damage is virtually completed.

DON'T CALL US--TURN ON RADIO OR TV

Snow or ice may necessitate closing schools for a day, delaying opening of school in the morning, or early closing of schools. Five days are provided in the calendar to allow for days when schools must be closed.

The decision on action to be taken because of inclement weather is made by Superintendent Davis after close checks of road conditions by our own transportation experts, as well as consultation with the police, highway and weather officials. The primary consideration is the safety of your children, and even though main roads may be clear the many secondary roads travelled by Fairfax County school buses are equally important in the final decision-making process.

The decision is made as early as possible and communicated quickly to all radio and television stations in the metropolitan area. So--if the weather looks bad turn on your radio or TV--the stations are most cooperative in carrying this information.

Please don't call a school or school administrative office for this information. The limited number of telephone lines are urgently needed for essential calls--such as notifying bus drivers of changed schedules.

ABOUT YOUR SCHOOL BOARD

Citizen control of public education in Fairfax County rests with an 11-member School Board, appointed by the Board of County Supervisors. Membership on the Board includes one member from each of the county's eight magisterial districts plus three at-large members, one of whom is a student.

The School Board meets in open session on the second and fourth Thursdays of each month at 8 p.m. Most meetings are held in the school administration building in Fairfax. Attend a Board meeting and see your School Board in action. For information about Board activities call 691-2291. Board members, their districts, and phone numbers are:

...Mrs. Mary Anne Lecos, chairman (Mason) (820-1124)
...Gene S. Bergoffen, vice chairman (Centreville) (471-5789)
...Mrs. Mona Blake (At-Large) (860-1028)
...John A. Christians (Annandale) (321-7880)
...Alfred S. Hodgson (Dranesville) (356-3146)
...Robert G. Hunt (At-Large) (461-9136)
...Mrs. Ann Kahn (Providence) (591-4589)
...Anthony T. Lane (Lee) (971-5946)
...T. Bradley Shipp (Student Member) (437-3880)
...Mrs. Marie B. Travesky (Springfield) (451-7135)
...Rufus W. Wright (Mount Vernon) (765-6682)

KNOW YOUR AREA SUPERINTENDENT

Because of its size, the Fairfax County Public School system is divided geographically into four administrative areas each headed by an area superintendent. Each area superintendent has direct supervision over about one-fourth of Fairfax County's 168 schools. As a matter of fact, each area is larger than most of the nation's school systems.

The area superintendent has a staff to assist him. Call your area superintendent if you have problems or questions which cannot be resolved by your local school. The area superintendents, their addresses and telephone numbers are:

...Area I--Taylor M. Williams, 3011 Memorial St., Alexandria (formerly Groveton Elementary School), 768-1122

...Area II--Joseph L. King, 6402 Franconia Rd., Springfield, in Key Intermediate School, 971-8200

...Area III--Barry Morris, 730A Marshall Road S.W., Vienna, in Marshall Road Elementary School, 938-6401

...Area IV--Donald Lacey, 10515 School St., Fairfax, in Eleven Oaks Annex, 591-6710

DIAL 691-2294 FOR SCHOOL NEWS

News about the Fairfax County Public Schools is recorded daily for your use--call 691-2294.

Figure 7-3 (Continued)

for your information

FAIRFAX COUNTY PUBLIC SCHOOLS
10700 Page Ave — Fairfax. Va 22030
GEORGE F. HAMEL
School Community Relations Director
PHONE: 691-2291

FOR IMMEDIATE RELEASE   September 21, 19

SCHOOL BOARD SUMMARY
Special Meeting, September 20, 1973

YEAR-ROUND EDUCATION

The School Board took the following action regarding the year-round education report which had

been presented by the staff on Sept. 6 and had been the subject of a workshop on Sept. 13.

... Directed the staff to continue the planning necessary for potential implementation of a pilot

study in one high school and its feeder intermediate and elementary schools in July 1975, with the

dual objectives of educational benefits and space utilization.

... Requested the staff to develop recommendations for more than one community for intensive

public communications dialogue. The staff was advised that before communities are selected the

Board will expect an outline of the scope and content of a communications package. This package is

to reflect a clear awareness of the requirement for responding to the basic questions that can be

expected regarding such matters as life-style, Board objectives, and extracurricular activities.

... Directed the staff to improve and expand the cost analysis of the pilot test.

... Requested the staff to concentrate on a study of the job opportunity situation at the high school

level.

... Committed itself to conducting a countywide public hearing on year-round education prior to

a final decision on implementation of a pilot study.

CONSTRUCTION MATTERS

The Board awarded a contract to M. C. Dean Electrical Contracting, Inc., in the amount of

$65,418 for installation of baseball field lighting systems at Oakton High School and Hayfield and

Robinson Secondary Schools. Multi-vapor light fixtures will be installed with underground wiring.

This is part of a program for installation of lighting at all county high schools with the School

Board funding football field lighting and the Board of Supervisors funding baseball field lighting.

A contract was also awarded to Jack Bays, Inc., in the amount of $201,700 for construction

of vehicle wash facilities at Newington and Jermantown maintenance centers. The cost of these

facilities will be jointly funded by the Board of Supervisors and the School Board.

A minor change was approved in the location of the easement at the Robinson Secondary

School site granted to the Virginia Electric Power Company last March for construction of a

power line.

Also approved was a deed of vacation for a road adjacent to Oakton High School. The owners

of property adjacent to the Oakton High site received approval from the Board of Supervisors for

(more)
A BACKGROUND SERVICE OF SCHOOL COMMUNITY RELATIONS

Figure 7-4

Page 2 / School Board Summary, September 21, 1973

vacating an existing road. School Board agreement was required since the road intersects a property line at Oakton High.

IN OTHER ACTION THE BOARD:

...Received recommendations from the Environmental Quality Advisory Council for the development of guidelines for implementation of the School Board's recently adopted environmental policy statement. These were referred to the staff for study and recommendation.

...Approved the appointment of Dr. Charles Davis, coordinator of media services, to represent the Board on the Fairfax County Library Board.

...Approved the addition of 44.5 personnel positions to maintain pupil/staff ratios based on the initial pupil membership report of September 7. Also approved was an additional aide position for a state-aided pilot program at Franklin Sherman Elementary School.

...Received an annual budget review for FY 1973 including the year-end status of all funds.

...Approved petty cash disbursements for the months of June and July.

...Approved a resolution to the Board of Supervisors requesting an increase of $642,013 in the fiscal plan and appropriation for FY 1973 undelivered orders outstanding.

...Received verbal opening-of-school reports from the four area superintendents.

...Received the annual report of the adult services program for the 1972-73 school year.

...Received a preliminary report from the Board committee studying Board procedures. Three workshops were scheduled for the development of Board objectives--on Oct. 29, Nov. 1, and Nov. 5.

...Received a report from the Superintendent that 117 high school seniors have been named as National Merit Scholarship semifinalists. All 20 of the county high schools having senior classes are represented (the new Lake Braddock and Chantilly Secondary Schools have students only in grades 7-10).

...Approved the recommendation of a majority of the fact-finding panel appointed to consider a grievance concerning the employee sick leave bank.

# # #

Figure 7-4 (Continued)

Welcome to

FAIRFAX COUNTY PUBLIC SCHOOLS

Information for Parents

The goal of the Fairfax County Public Schools is to accept the responsibility for the development of each child into an adult who can stand confidently, participate fully, learn continually, and contribute meaningfully in his world.

This includes a commitment to provide quality education and equality of opportunity for all students.

1973-74 Student Calendar

Aug. 8-9   Registration for new students

(Families arriving later register on arrival. Register at school serving area in which student resides. This information available by calling 691-2833.)

Sept. 4	First day of school
Oct. 8	Columbus Day holiday
Oct. 22	Veterans Day holiday
Nov. 8-9	Student holiday
Nov. 22-23	Thanksgiving holiday
Dec. 24-Jan. 1	Christmas holiday
Jan. 28	Student holiday
Jan. 29	Second semester begins
Feb. 18	Washington's Day holiday
Apr. 5	Student holiday
Apr. 8-12	Spring holiday
May 27	Memorial Day holiday
June 13	Last day of school

Education-- A Public Responsibility

Citizen control of public education rests with the 11-member School Board, appointed by the elected Board of County Supervisors. As part of the county government structure, there is one Board member for each of eight magisterial (election) districts plus three at-large members, one of whom is a student.

Regularly scheduled public meetings are held the second and fourth Thursdays of each month at 8 p.m., generally in the School Administration Building, 10700 Page Ave., Fairfax. Agendas and summaries of Board actions are available on request.

The Board in Action

Primary function of the School Board is to develop policies, written statements of intent guiding operation of the school program. These policies, as well as regulations and notices, are placed in two loose-leaf volumes maintained in each school for citizen inspection.

BOARD MEMBERS (with telephones)

Chairman
Mrs. Mary Anne Lecos, Mason (820-1124)*

Vice Chairman
Gene S. Bergoffen, Centreville (471-5789)*

Mrs. Mona Blake, At-Large (860-1028)*
John A. Christians, Annandale (321-7880)**
Alfred S. Hodgson, Dranesville (356-3146)*
Robert G. Hunt, At-Large (461-9136)*
Mrs. Ann Kahn, Providence (591-4589)**
Anthony T. Lane, Lee (971-5946)*
Thomas Bradley Shipp, Student Member (437-3880)**
Mrs. Marie B. Travesky, Springfield (451-7135)**
Rufus W. Wright, Mount Vernon (765-6682)**

*Term expires Dec. 31, 1973
**Term expires June 30, 1974

Figure 7-5

Carrying Out Policies

Chief executive officer of the Fairfax County School Board is the Division Superintendent, appointed for a four-year term. The Division Superintendent has an immediate staff to interpret and carry out Board policies.

The county school system has been divided into four geographic areas of about equal population, each containing approximately 40 schools. An area superintendent and his staff are located in offices in the area. Area administration is the arm of the Division Superintendent at the local level where problems may be more easily identified and solved. Area offices implement instructional and pupil service programs. They also evaluate principals, select and counsel personnel, and facilitate budgeting, transportation, maintenance, plant operation and food services. For further information on area organization, request brochure from local school or call 691-2291.

The evolving role of central administration encompasses development of objectives, of a work program to achieve them, of performance indicators, and evaluation. Instruction and curriculum are centrally developed, carried out through areas. Major responsibilities of central administration include thrust and direction for such other programs and services as personnel career development and employee relations, business affairs, support services, research, construction, planning, and communications.

SCHOOL ADMINISTRATION

Dr. S. John Davis is Division Superintendent. His staff includes associate superintendents for instructional and personnel services and for instructional support; assistant superintendents for instructional services, personnel, business affairs, support services, and educational facilities planning and construction; a coordinator of human relations; a director of planning and program assessment; a director of administrative services; and a director of school-community relations.

Some Indices of Quality

Parents hold high aspirations for their children. Some 73 percent of the approximately 9,200 graduates in June 1973 are going on to some form of post-secondary education, about 56 percent of them to four-year colleges and universities.

Countywide testing is conducted in grades K, 2, 4, 6, 8, 9, and 11. Results in reading, mathematics, science, language arts, and social studies show students generally scoring significantly higher than national norms on standardized tests. For further information on testing, request brochure from local school or call 691-2291.

Students have earned honors and awards in all basic subject areas in regional, state and national competition.

All schools are accredited by the State Board of Education and the Southern Association of Colleges and Schools. Continued accreditation involves periodic reevaluation. Southern Association requires reevaluation by committees of outside educators as well as self-study by the principal and his staff.

Parents and citizens are committed to adequate financial support of schools. Two of every three dollars collected in local taxes are earmarked for school purposes. Local revenue sources provide about 70 percent of school operating costs of $155.2 million. State sources account for approximately 21 percent and federal sources about 9 percent. It is estimated that the cost of education for each student for 1973-74 will be $1,154.

(For general information call the Department of School-Community Relations, 691-2291, or the appropriate area office—Area I, 768-1122; Area II, 971-8200; Area III, 938-6401 or 938-1957; Area IV, 591-6710.)

Figure 7-5 (Continued)

About Fairfax County Public Schools

The Nation's 15th largest system, Fairfax County Public Schools projects an enrollment for 1973-74 of 135,721, preschool through grade 12—in 168 schools (128 elementary, K-6; 18 intermediate, 7-8; 18 high, 9-12; 4 secondary, 7-12).

Attendance is compulsory in Virginia between sixth and seventeenth birthdays. School law requires that schools be in session a minimum of 180 days. To enroll in kindergarten for 1973-74 school year (classes in all elementary schools), children must reach their fifth birthday on or before Nov. 1, or, to enter first-year primary, their sixth birthday on or before Oct. 1. Continuous progress, rather than traditional annual automatic moves from one grade level to the next, assures that kindergarten children will move ahead to the full extent of their abilities.

To enroll a student, parents visit the school office, taking with them student birth certificate or equivalent (this is required) and a transfer slip or report card forwarded with the family from previous school. Physical examinations and certain immunizations are required for pupils entering school for the first time. (For information, call the Fairfax County Health Department, 691-3141.) Dental examinations are highly recommended. The Health Department provides such support as health screening and nursing services in the schools.

Reports to parents on academic performance of students are rendered quarterly. Grading periods end Nov. 7, Jan. 25, Apr. 4, June 13.

Children are assigned to elementary schools serving the area in which they reside; secondary schools serve wider geographic areas embracing several feeder schools. Because of shifting enrollments, varying school capacities and program requirements, and new construction, individual school boundaries are adjusted periodically. Adjustments are made annually for the following school year; parents are notified in advance. Exceptions to adopted attendance areas are permitted only by School Board action, following application which may be submitted at the local school.

Bus transportation is provided for elementary school students who live more than one mile from school; intermediate and high school students who live more than one and one-half miles away, and for students who would have to walk on hazardous routes.

Textbooks are provided free. School stores sell at minimum cost supplies, vocational-related items, gym clothing, and enrichment materials. School accident insurance is optional, as are certain fees associated with school activities.

Nutritious lunches are served in every school. Some schools also have a breakfast program.

Inclement weather may result in closing schools, delayed opening, or early dismissal. Radio and television stations carry this news as soon as such decisions are made; parents are urged not to call local school or administrative offices.

Individual school opening and closing hours are developed by the principal. Minimum daily hours are: kindergarten, 3; elementary, 6 including lunch period; intermediate, 6 hours, 15 minutes including lunch period; high school, 6½ hours including lunch. In order to provide time for staff development, curriculum development, and teacher conferences with parents and students, arrangements can be made by the principal working with the area superintendent to close school early. Generally these early closings are on Mondays but can be held on other days to accommodate special activities. Parents will be informed through their schools of operating schedules.

Work permits, mandatory for youth under 18 who seek employment, are issued at individual high schools.

Telephone numbers for all schools and area and central administrative offices are listed in the Virginia Suburban Section of the C&P Telephone directory under "Fairfax County Public Schools."

Figure 7-5 (Continued)

THE KINDERGARTEN CHILD

—is curious

—manipulates objects

—explores his environment

—experiments

KINDERGARTEN

THE FIRST STEP

Kindergarten for most children is the beginning of a planned program which focuses on the interests and unique educational needs of young children. Kindergarten instruction is designed to:

—build a foundation in basic skills

—stress oral language skills

—extend intellectual potentials through a variety of experiences

—encourage social skills

—improve perceptual motor skills

Figure 7-6

THE KINDERGARTEN TEACHER

—assesses achievement

—diagnoses in order to plan instruction

—observes and records behaviors

—fosters a positive attitude and opportunities for successful learning

—designs and structures the classroom environment

—organizes each day's activities

—uses direct teaching of small groups as well as questioning of individuals as they work at learning centers

THE KINDERGARTEN CLASSROOM

—is a learning laboratory capitalizing on a child's curiosity

—is organized into many centers

listening
language arts
art
housekeeping
blocks
library
music
mathematics
social studies
construction
science

—is changed at intervals in response to instructional needs

Figure 7-6 (Continued)

THE KINDERGARTEN CURRICULUM

—provides for active involvement

—emphasizes basic skills

pre-reading and reading
language
mathematics
science
social studies
art
music
construction

—develops perceptual motor skills

—fosters development of curiosity and creativity

—fosters interaction with peers and adults

—fosters self-awareness

—extends experience in the expressive arts

—operates on a continuous progress learning program

GENERAL INFORMATION

—Registration for kindergarten is done in the local elementary school; for information on the school serving your address, call 691-2833.

—An orientation meeting for parents, and preschool screening for prospective kindergarten students, is scheduled by each school, usually in the spring.

—At the beginning and end of the regular school day, kindergarten children either ride regular school buses or walk to and from school with older children under safety patrol supervision; at mid-day, bus transportation is provided for all kindergarten children unless they live adjacent to the school.

—A mid-morning and mid-afternoon snack may be purchased at the school. Kindergarten schedule assumes that the child will have lunch at home.

—The kindergarten class day is three hours, either morning or afternoon.

—There is an average of 25 children to a class.

—Reports to parents on the child's progress occur regularly.

—Detailed information on kindergarten program is available from the school. School phone numbers are listed under "Fairfax County" in the phone book.

—Children must be five years old on or before Nov. 1, 1973, to enroll for kindergarten for the 1973-74 school year; must be five on or before Dec. 1, 1974, for the 1974-75 school year; and five on or before Jan. 1, 1976, for the 1975-76 session. To enter first grade, the child must be six on or before Oct. 1, 1973, for the 1973-74 school year; six on or before Nov. 1, 1974, for 1974-75; and six on or before Dec. 1, 1975, for 1975-76 session, and six on or before Jan. 1, 1976, for the 1976-77 session. These are requirements of state law.

INFORMATION MEMO #1–1973-4
FAIRFAX COUNTY PUBLIC SCHOOLS
10700 Page Avenue
Fairfax, Va. 22030

Figure 7-6 (Continued)

INFORMATION ABOUT STANDARDIZED TEST SCORES

Standardized tests, developed for nationwide use, are used by Fairfax County Public Schools to identify strengths and weaknesses of curriculum and of individual students, and to plan needed improvements.

The chart inside reflects achievement and ability in terms of national norms. The percentile of 50 represents the average percentile for the nation.

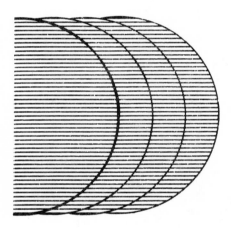

FAIRFAX COUNTY PUBLIC SCHOOLS FAIRFAX, VA.   22030

INFORMATION MEMO #2   1972-73   FAIRFAX COUNTY PUBLIC SCHOOLS

THE TESTS USED 1971-72

METROPOLITAN READINESS TESTS—Given to all kindergarten students

INTELLIGENCE TEST (Lorge-Thorndike)— Given to all 4th and 6th graders

MENTAL MATURITY TEST (California)— Given to all 7th graders

ACHIEVEMENT TEST (SRA)—Given to all 4th and 6th graders

SILENT READING TESTS (Iowa)—Given to all 7th graders

APTITUDE AND ACHIEVEMENT TESTS (SCAT-STEP)—Given to 9th and 11th graders in many high schools

COLLEGE BOARD Aptitude and Achievement Tests—taken by 9,445 students planning to attend college. Aptitude tests were taken by 4,851 seniors and 4,594 juniors. Numbers taking achievement tests varied from 2,570 seniors (composition) to 24 seniors (European history and world cultures)

Figure 7-7

WHAT IS MEASURED?

Development of key skills necessary for academic success

Scholastic aptitude

Scholastic aptitude

Overall achievement, as well as achievement in areas of social studies, science, language arts, arithmetic, reading, study skills

Proficiency in work-study reading

General aptitude, plus achievement in reading, spelling, capitalization and punctuation, mechanics and effectiveness of writing, mathematics, computation and concepts, science, social studies (9th grade); and mathematics, science, reading, writing (11th grade)

Student's knowledge of a specific subject and his ability to solve problems related to it. (Tests are designed to sample what is taught in a wide variety of schools, not just those with a particular curriculum or teaching method)

HOW OUR CHILDREN COMPARED IN 1971-72

In 1972, average kindergartner in FCPS outperformed 79% of the children in the national norm group

In grade 4, average performance was better than 63% of the national norm group, in grade 6, better than 75% in the national norm group

The average performance of Fairfax County children was better than 73% of children in the national norm group

The average Fairfax County child ranks above 63% of the national norm group in 4th grade, and 60% in 6th grade. Fairfax County students compare with the national norms of 50 as follows:

Grade	Social Studies	Science	Lang. Arts	Arithmetic	Reading
4	65	61	59	66	68
6	55	59	56	57	65

Average Fairfax County student scored above 66/ of national norm group

In the aptitude test, the average Fairfax County student tested scored above 60% of the national norm group in 9th grade, 70% in 11th grade. The average 9th grader taking the achievement tests scored above these percents of the national norm group: reading, 63; spelling, 50; capitalization and punctuation, 45; mechanics of writing, 50; effectiveness of writing, 59; mathematics computation, 58; science, 59; social studies, 56. Those in grade 11 scored above these percents of the national norm group: mathematics, 65; science, 62; reading, 66; writing, 70

Compared to other college-bound students around the nation, FCPS test takers ranked outstandingly higher in European history, physics, Spanish; near or slightly above national norms on verbal and math aptitude, composition, literature, American history, Math II, biology, French, German; slightly below on Math I, chemistry, Latin

Figure 7-7 (Continued)

TRENDS IN TEST RESULTS

While the superior performance of Fairfax County students in comparison with other school divisions within the state has been maintained or improved over the past year, there has been a general slight decline in recent years in Fairfax County as well as throughout Virginia in achievement test results at both 4th and 6th grade levels relative to the national norm. The rate of decline last year was slower than in the two prior years.

WHAT IS BEING DONE TO IMPROVE TEST RESULTS?

It is generally agreed that a student's scores on achievement batteries are the net result of what has been learned both in school and outside of school. The school system has the responsibility to take action to reverse any decline in results that may be attributable to in-school experiences.

Fairfax County Public Schools has taken steps to improve learning in fields where a need has been identified as a result of analysis of achievement tests in recent years; the slowing in rate of test score decline may be the result of these steps. It will take several years, though, before any clear-cut changes in test scores can be attributed to such action.

Among the steps taken to improve the learning situation in general, as well as to reverse the decline in achievement test score results, are these:

—Using data collected by a FCPS program of testing kindergarten children, first grade teachers have been given advance notification about specific children who may need special attention in order to succeed.

—A diagnostic testing program is provided to elementary schools for use in developing ways of helping pupils who score low on achievement tests.

—Detailed analysis of test results has identified the specific areas of curriculum strengths and weaknesses of FCPS children. This information has been provided administrators and specialists responsible for these parts of the curriculum; this may lead to recommendations for curriculum changes, or to shifts in areas of emphasis.

—A program of compensatory education involving special assistance to schools having more than the average number of under-achieving students has been instituted for the 1972-73 school year, with reading specialists assigned to these schools, and inservice training for kindergarten teachers.

—A statistical study has been initiated on all items of the STEP achievement test administered to the 9th and 11th graders in the fall of 1972. These findings, like the analysis of the 4th and 6th grade results, will be submitted to administrators and curriculum specialists for appropriate action.

—Alternative programs and organizations are being studied as a means of improving student competencies.

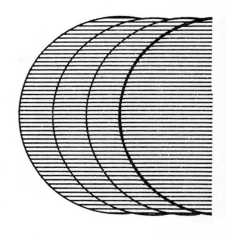

For further information on standardized tests, contact your school's principal, or, for information concerning the entire county, contact Division of Research & Testing, Dept. of Instructional Services, Fairfax County Public Schools, 6402 Franconia Rd., Springfield, Va. 22150.

Figure 7-7 (Continued)

PREPARING THE MESSAGE

Some of the vehicles and methods of communicating the message have been discussed under planning. However, a vital key is the message itself.

Preparing the message is too important a task to entrust solely to educators. Whenever possible, a professional communicator should be utilized. Allowing the professional educator to prepare the material by himself may result in a profusion of "educationese" which will turn off the audience. The public, already suspicious and critical of educators, will probably reject the message outright.

Teachers, principals, and other administrators should certainly make the major substantive contribution to preparing information. However, professional communicators within the school system, if any, should play a key role.

Community involvement should also be included in message preparation, with the establishment of a communications committee or task force strongly recommended. This task force should include students and community leaders, as well as staff personnel. Particularly valuable resources for membership are professional communicators who may live within the school district, are interested in education, and may even have children in the schools. These may include persons employed in the following occupations: public relations, radio/television work, newspaper work, and professional writing. Media organizations are recognizing the public relations value of their employees, participating in community efforts such as this.

In preparing the message, a valuable term or slogan to use as a test and as a principle to follow is one frequently used in teaching effective writing: "KISS" or "Keep it simple, stupid." Another good rule is that followed in news writing: Write at the sixth grade level if you expect the public really to "listen" to your message.

While written material must be an important part of the program, the old adage that "a good picture is worth 1,000 words" should be kept in mind. Good visual and sound aids are highly important for use in all phases of the program. Examples of materials that will be needed are professional-caliber tapes, slides, and transparencies for use by speakers; video-tapes, films, and filmstrips; and photographs.

EVALUATING THE COMMUNICATIONS PROGRAM

A noted educator in public relations is fond of saying, "If you are a public relations man, and your boss sends for you and demands an evaluation of the effect of your program, your best course of action is to create a dramatic diversion to get his mind off the subject." While this is obviously an exaggeration, and considerable progress has been made in recent years in evaluating the effectiveness of communications programs, such evaluation is at best an imprecise art.

There are organizations that specialize in opinion surveys of education, and they are obviously best equipped to really find out what people think about curriculum change; and to determine where your communications program has succeeded, where it has failed, and where future effort should be channeled. This process is time-consuming and expensive, but it is probably the best way of determining public attitudes without the bias of what staff people "think" the public attitudes are. If possible, surveying should be done before, during, and after communicating.

Of course one of the best evaluations of the communication program is the degree of public acceptance of curriculum improvement programs. It should be remembered that the average citizen does not really care about something new unless or until it affects him or his family, but he can be a "tiger" if he feels he or his children are threatened by something that he doesn't fully understand.

Some evaluation can be accomplished at the local school district level by telephone surveys, questionnaires, public reaction at meetings, and other techniques. Some difficulties involved where professional or experienced survey personnel are not available include: constructing the survey instrument to be sure it is free of bias and measures what is sought; and, most critical of all, selecting the sample to ensure that it represents the entire population. It should include the silent majority and not be limited to activists and opinion leaders. The limitations of such surveys should be clearly recognized to ensure that the true reaction, rather than the hoped-for reaction, is obtained.

8

The Student and Curriculum Improvement

The student of all ages can and should contribute to the improvement of the curriculum in which he participates. Every educator is aware that, aided and abetted by the current wave of individual freedom, and supported in many instances by the courts and liberal groups, students have demanded and received greater freedom of choice and action, often including the right to accept or reject the instruction offered by their schools. This chapter discusses:

(1) the legitimate role of students in curriculum improvement,
(2) student rights and responsibilities in this area, and
(3) student accountability for the curriculum improvement process.

THE ROLE OF THE STUDENT IN CURRICULUM IMPROVEMENT

Curriculum improvement activities take place at four levels: the district level, the school level, the classroom level, and the individual learner level. The student can and should participate in varying degrees at all four levels. This participation falls into three categories:

(1) information roles,
(2) advisory roles, and
(3) decision-making roles.

Generally speaking, student participation should be largely informational and advisory at the district and school level, with increasing responsibility for decision-making at the classroom and individual student level. Although there may be desirable variations, the role of the student may be represented as shown in Figure 8-1.

STUDENT ROLE IN CURRICULUM IMPROVEMENT

Level of Activity	Student Role		
District	Information	Limited Advisory	————————
School	Information	Advisory	Limited Decision-Making
Class	Information	Advisory	Limited Decision-Making
Individual Student	Information	Advisory	Decision-Making

Figure 8-1

Each of these roles will be discussed in general terms without attempting to provide for the wide range of ages covered and the resulting differences in kinds and extent of participation. However, in this chapter we are concerned with elementary and secondary students only.

Information Role of the Student

Students of any age can participate meaningfully in curriculum improvement by providing information to curriculum planners. This information should never be of the "spying" type, nor should it be secretive. Rather, by serving on various committees and participating in discussion groups, students can provide insights into matters such as:

— pupil satisfactions and dissatisfactions
— pupil out-of-school needs
— pupil career plans
— desired courses
— effectiveness of new programs
— reasons for pupil unrest
— student-teacher relationships
— effective techniques
— pupil-desired changes
— degree of pupil participation in planning

The administrator should review this information thoughtfully and carefully, and it should serve as one of the many sources of information contributing to the curriculum improvement process. It will provide valuable insights into the validity of using students in the advisory or decision-making roles.

The key administrator should utilize such information to assist in planning at the district level. In addition, it is his responsibility to see that principals and teachers provide for student information input during their curriculum improvement programs. Information about students *provided by students* becomes increasingly important as the focus of curriculum improvement moves from the school to the teacher, and to the individual teacher-learner activity. This fact must be recognized and must become a part of the day-to-day instructional program if, in fact, student involvement is to be useful in curriculum improvement. A day-to-day operation that recognizes the importance of student input is a prerequisite to meaningful student input during the improvement process.

The Advisory Role of the Student

School districts and schools are using increasing numbers of students in an advisory capacity, either as individuals, student advisory groups, or as student representatives serving on advisory committees. Where such advisory participation has proven effective, the following conditions have existed:

— a meaningful role has been established and defined—the student appointments have not been "window dressing."

— the committee or function has been established prior to a problem occurring, not as a "clean up" activity.

— adult members have truly wanted student participation.

— the student knows his role in advance with advisory and decision-making roles having been carefully identified.

— at the individual school level, student groups have been charged with the responsibility for solving real problems and dealing with issues of substance.

— adult guidance has been provided—kindly and patient, but firm.

The preceding conditions relate primarily to participation at the district and school level. It is the responsibility of the administration and principals to see that classroom planning, individual career counseling, and course selection include advisory student input. As in the case of the informational role, the advisory role of the student is critical at the individual student level, and, if widely employed throughout a school, it will result in meaningful and effective schoolwide curriculum improvement.

Districtwide student advisory councils can prove quite effective and are used by many school administrators in a communications and advisory role. Their roles include a variety of responsibilities. They are usually limited to students at the secondary school level. Their existence, functions, composition, and method of operation should be made a part of official school board policy, either in the district's policy manual, its statement of students' rights and responsibilities, or other appropriate school district records. As an example, the school board regulation establishing a student advisory council for Fairfax County, Virginia, is reproduced in Figure 8-2.

Regulation 2300.
August 6, 1971

Section 4 *Student Advisory Council*

The Student Advisory Council shall be composed of one elected representative from each high school. This representative shall be

Figure 8-2

chosen annually from the membership of that school's delegation to the Area Advisory Council.

School Board meeting agendas and summaries will be provided to all members of the Student Advisory Council and background materials for Board meeting subjects will be given to the chairman of the SAC on particular items at his request. Representatives designated by the SAC would be welcome to appear before the Board from time to time to comment on specific agenda items of interest to the SAC and to submit their views in writing on any subject.

The *Student Advisory Council* shall elect its own officers. It has the power to adopt bylaws as necessary to fulfill its purposes.

Each administrative area will have an *Area Student Advisory Council* whose purpose is similar to that of the *County Council.* Selection of the Area Council members will be as follows:

1. Each Council shall be composed of an equal number of students from each high school.
2. Underclassmen shall comprise one-half of the representation.
3. The method for choosing representatives shall be determined by the student government at each school.

Diagram of Organization

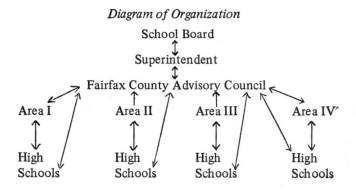

Arrows indicate interaction among the various groups and individuals.

Figure 8-2[1] (Continued)

---

[1]Reproduced from *Responsibilities and Rights: Secondary School Students,* Fairfax County Public Schools, Fairfax, Virginia, January, 1973.

The student advisory committee created by the regulation has worked with varying degrees of effectiveness. In fact, in large measure, the conditions for effective participation described are based upon observations of the group in action.

This group, frequently working with the student member of the school board, has been instrumental in the development of "The Students' Rights and Responsibility Manual" and its adoption as school board policy, the initiation of pass-fail courses in some curriculum areas, the changing of regulations regarding smoking privileges, and the development of a student assembly organization which has recommended the student school board appointee.

The Decision-Making Role of the Student

The role of the student in making decisions as to what, when, how, and by whom he should be taught is a controversial one. Opinions run the gamut. In Fairfax County, Virginia, student board of education member has full voting privileges and receives the same compensation as other board members. Students have run for board posts in districts where it is an elected office, and some have been elected. Other school districts feel that students are not capable of making any kind of decisions, including dealing with what their individual educational program should be. As the administrator attempts to provide for meaningful student participation in the decision-making process, the following guidelines are pertinent:

- in most instances, the superintendent and school board are legally responsible for the educational program at the district level. They cannot ignore or delegate this responsibility.
- the principal is assigned the educational leadership responsibility at the individual school. In most instances, decision-making (as opposed to being heard and advising) for curriculum improvement is the responsibility of adults, not students.
- limited participation in decision-making at the school and classroom level is both appropriate and desirable. The same operating rules as those identified at the advisory level should be followed.
- the individual student, as he matures, should have an increasing voice in curriculum and the choice of what he will participate in. However, adult

    guidance both at school and at home is essential if he is to make wise decisions and choices.

— in the classroom setting, the student should participate in establishing reasonable goals for himself. At the high school level, this should include a voice in the selection and improving of courses.

The key administrator should recognize that learning takes place on an individual basis, and curriculum improvement has occurred only when the learning experiences of individual students have been improved. He must ensure that staff and teachers embrace this concept as a goal in the curriculum improvement process. It is unreasonable to assume that the individual student should have no voice in what his learning experiences shall be. It is equally ridiculous to assume that he should have complete control over selecting all of these experiences. The key administrator should develop the appropriate level of student participation at all ages in the informational, advisory, and decision-making aspects of curriculum improvement.

STUDENT RIGHTS AND RESPONSIBILITIES FOR CURRICULUM IMPROVEMENT

Many school districts are developing student rights and responsibility statements and booklets. This movement has included varying degrees of student participation in curriculum decisions. The Fairfax County, Virginia policy includes the following statement outlining one role of student government in this way:

> The student government shall work to see that the purposes of the school are fulfilled and to improve communication among students, teachers, parents and school officials. School officials are encouraged to consult with student government on matters of curriculum, procedures, faculty-student relations and discipline.[2]

The development of student rights and responsibility state-

---

[2]Fairfax County Schools, *Responsibilities and Rights: Secondary School Students,* Fairfax County Schools, January, 1973.

ments provide an excellent vehicle for defining an appropriate role for students in the curriculum improvement process.

The key administrator should see that their responsibilities in curriculum improvement are clearly defined. The responsibility of students to work toward a school environment conducive to improving the instructional opportunities of all students should be a definite part of any student code.

STUDENT ACCOUNTABILITY FOR CURRICULUM IMPROVEMENT

Today's educational accountability statements and practices usually stop with the teacher. Students can and should be held accountable for their performances and the results attained. In most instances, they are willing and expect to be accountable if the procedures are fair. How often we have heard students say, "He's a tough teacher, but he is fair and impartial. He's my best teacher."

This fact is illustrated by the following quotation from a taped interview with a Fairfax County high school student:

I think it's important that we distinquish between discipline in the classroom and discipline in the school as a whole, as perhaps the administration would discipline the students. In order to carry on a good classroom situation there must be discipline, and it's up to the teacher to discipline the students. However, the students also have a responsibility to themselves and to their classmates to maintain good discipline whatever the schedule, whatever the teacher wants carried on. Discipline in the school is an individual's responsibility to himself to maintain some sort of order in the school so things can be accomplished—not only the educational processes but also social activities and other things that make school more enjoyable for the students.

. . .

However, it is important that the goals of the administration concerning discipline be made clear at the beginning and throughout the school year, so that students know when they are carrying on activities that are outside what is expected of them as far as discipline in the school is concerned.[3]

[3]Fairfax County, Virginia, Public Schools, *Fairfax Schools Bulletin,* Volume 10, No. 2, Fairfax County Schools, October, 1973.

The key administrator should include students in the development of curriculum improvement projects so that they are aware of what is expected, and can participate in developing goals that are meaningful, useful and attainable. The student can then be held accountable for his performance—good, bad, or indifferent.

The student should be held accountable in two major areas:

(1) His support and contribution to a school that provides desirable educational opportunities, as mentioned in previous sections.
(2) His performance in school, based upon realistically established goals that are related to his ability, experience, interests, and personal characteristics.

It is the responsibility of all concerned with the curriculum improvement process to see that the goals of curriculum improvement projects take these factors into account. If students are allowed and encouraged to participate in the planning and development stages of the curriculum improvement effort, they can then be held accountable for a reasonable level of performance once programs are implemented.

9

Working with the Board of Education, Community Groups, and Outside Resources

Today's school administrators must work with many persons and groups of persons who are not employees of the school district and not subject to its rules and policies. Working with several of the most important of these is discussed in this chapter—local boards of education, citizens and citizens' groups, professional organizations, consultants, and state departments of education.

LOCAL BOARD OF EDUCATION

As the educational policy-making body in the district, the board of education has the responsibility and authority to direct its attention to matters of curriculum and instruction. The superintendent of schools or the key administrator of the curriculum improvement project, if not the superintendent, needs board understanding and support for projects contemplated or underway. Much has been written about educator relations with the board of education. However, the following guidelines for working with the board, while in most instances applying to all board-educator relations, seem particularly important in relation to curriculum improvement efforts:

(1) Try to establish a dividing line between policy and administration in the curriculum improvement process delineating the roles of the board and of the staff.

(2) Explain the curriculum improvement plan and project to the board.

(3) Don't be possessive of the program improvement area—let the board in on the act.

(4) Free the board to work on curriculum improvement and see that individual members are given active, meaningful assignments.

(5) Recognize and admit weaknesses of current programs—be objective and build that image of the staff.

(6) Don't oversell by promising too much, too fast. Don't guarantee success; at least allow for partial failure or limited success.

(7) Try to establish the fact that improvements cost money and require time, training, and resources.

(8) Forward materials to the board well in advance of decision-making whenever possible.

(9) Don't spring surprises—anticipate trouble spots.

An effective board of education's role in curriculum improvement is difficult to establish. The board, on the one hand, must set instructional policy but, on the other hand, the staff has teachers and specialists who are experts in their academic fields. Membership on boards changes rapidly, and the staff frequently finds itself "educating" a new board or board members. Board members may come to the board with political orientations and preconceived plans for change. In the absence of a systematic plan for communicating with and providing orientation for school board members, they may become liabilities rather than an asset in the curriculum improvement process.

A consortium of twenty-seven South Carolina school districts undertook the preparation of both superintendents and school board members for curriculum improvement efforts and improved communications through a series of seminars, workshops, and visitations to exemplary or innovative educational programs. This program sought (1) to assist school board members and superintendents in defining their distinct and unique roles in the educational improvement process, and (2) to provide a framework under which school board members could establish policies that would produce more effective school programs.

Consultants were utilized to present the seminars and worksnops which were devoted to:

(1) "The Role of Education in the Present Day Culture"
(2) "The Role of School Boards in Education Today"
(3) "The Changes in the Culture of South Carolina with the Economic Shift of Emphasis from Agriculture to Industry"
(4) "The Implications of Economic and Industrial Change for School Curriculum"
(5) "General Curriculum—Kindergarten Through Senior High School"
(6) "Vocational Education"
(7) "Adult Education"
(8) "Educational Policy-Making and Administrative Decision-Making."

This group of school board members and superintendents visited selected exemplary pre-elementary, middle, and secondary schools where they had the opportunity to meet and talk with resident administrators, teachers, and board members. Also included were visits to a vocational program for handicapped students, a boys' school, a school emphasizing individualized instruction, and a school devoted to the performing arts and cultural development (North Carolina School of the Arts in Winston-Salem).

This rather ambitious program for superintendents and school board members will continue to pay off in future years. More modest efforts along these lines could be pursued by individual school districts or as a joint effort by school districts on a regional basis. However, the turnover of superintendents and board members requires continued efforts to ensure effective teamwork for educational improvement.

Techniques for Communicating with the School Board

All meetings of the staff and school board, whether they be regular board meetings, work sessions, or informal discussions, provide opportunities for communicating with the board. Among the techniques that have been used in one or more of these settings are the following:

(1) Holding meetings in schools.
(2) Furnishing board members with nationally, state, and locally produced curriculum publications.
(3) Having a short staff presentation on curriculum at each meeting.
(4) Giving visual presentations.
(5) Including board members on curriculum improvement committees and workshops.
(6) Using consultants with the board.
(7) Devoting specific work sessions to curriculum evaluation and improvement.
(8) Exploring alternate approaches to curriculum improvement—identifying as many as possible—perhaps including some that may seem unreasonable.
(9) Admitting, "I don't know," or "The staff doesn't have the answer."
(10) Using the board meeting as a communications device by including information items as well as action items.
  — give support for the point of view expressed—discuss alternates.
  — provide back-up information in written form.
  — have information sessions in all curriculum areas, especially potentially troublesome areas, prior to anticipated difficulties.
  — include "information only" items in board meeting materials—this adds some status and ensures reading.
(11) Making presentations to the board by superintendent, staff, principals, and teachers. When making presentations the following guidelines are helpful:
  — rehearse and plan.
  — be brief and to the point.
  — support recommendations by statistics, and illustrations.
  — include knowledgeable staff members—don't "hog the show."
  — use visual aids and media presentations.
  — include students, if at all suitable.
  — give the board basic materials beforehand so they are ready and do not have to take notes.
  — whenever possible, give items to the board several meetings in advance of action.
(12) Using the budget and the budget-making process as communicating devices. The budget review process provides an opportunity to discuss

curriculum and instructional programs as well as funds and finance. Using a program budgeting format will facilitate this type of discussion. Even with a traditional line item budget, the superintendent and his staff should be prepared to discuss the curriculum and instructional programs. (See Chapter 11.)

CITIZEN PARTICIPATION

Increased citizen participation in educational affairs is a fact of life in our present society. This participation may be positive, constructive, and beneficial to the educational program of the school or district; or it may be militant, demanding, negative, and destructive to good educational practice. The situation is further complicated by the fact that opinions differ widely as to what is positive and what is negative. This difference of opinion may be between the school and citizens or citizens' groups; or it may be between groups of citizens. The administrator and curriculum improver must make every effort to utilize citizen interest and concern to improve the educational opportunities provided by the school or school district.

Types of Citizen Participation

The following list of citizen participants, though by no means exhaustive, illustrates the wide range of citizen involvement and interest in the educational decision-making process. These categories are not mutually exclusive and no attempt has been made to make them so:

(1) P.T.A.'s—Citizen Associations—Booster Clubs—Parent groups.
(2) Standing advisory committees for special education, vocational education, etc.
(3) Members of student-parent-staff study groups.
(4) Ad hoc task forces on bond issues, goals and objectives, and study of specific problem areas.
(5) Groups providing survey information.
(6) Resource persons in the curriculum improvement process.

(7) Readers and consumers of media—newspapers, radio, T.V.
(8) Readers and consumers of materials that schools send home.
(9) Individual parents.
(10) Citizen pressure groups:
  — Taxpayers' groups to lower taxes.
  — Special interest groups; e.g., music, art, physical education, and special education.
  — "Anti" groups; e.g., groups against sex education, groups against permissiveness, groups against "frills."
  — Community sponsored athletic groups; e.g., Police Youth Leagues, little leagues, soccer.
  — Building use groups.
  — Ethnic and minority pressure groups.

The administrator should utilize citizens in as many positive ways as possible; i.e., as members of advisory committees, study groups, ad hoc task force groups, and resource committees. Selections to such groups should be made carefully; limits of authority and advisory functions carefully defined; job tasks for the group clearly defined; tenure of service established; staff liaison and support provided; and procedures established for dissemination, consideration, and possible adoption of recommendations delineated. All of these matters should be clearly established before work begins.

Effective involvement of citizens in educational planning and decision-making will not occur naturally. In most school districts, such involvement represents a new endeavor, not only for citizens but also for educational administrators, requiring the definition of roles, functions, and responsibilities. Fairfax County, Virginia, has approached the involvement of the community through cooperative seminars for educational administrators and citizens. An important outgrowth of this cooperation has been the establishment of operational "education committees" in several schools where citizens (usually parents, but also businessmen, medical personnel, clergymen, law enforcement personnel, and civic leaders) work with the principal in determining problem areas, suggesting possible areas for program improvement, and evaluating the school program.

Working with Citizen Pressure Groups

Citizen groups often organize to exert pressure on the administration and school board to achieve their ends. Their objectives are usually commendable and worthwhile, though this may not always be true. Working with pressure groups may be a difficult and frustrating task, especially if the board and administration agree with their basic aims but do not have necessary funds, facilities, or personnel, or feel that implementation of their aims would imbalance or overload the total program in a specific program area. In many instances, these groups can become dynamic forces that bring about desired improvements and innovations. The administrator must guide their efforts in positive directions. The following suggestions have proved useful in working with pressure groups:

(1) Have an established policy whenever possible.
(2) Have your board share the burden.
(3) Listen courteously and as objectively as possible—they may be right and they may have legislation and the courts on their side.
(4) Include these people on existing committees.
(5) Keep a record of meetings, calls, concerns, etc.
(6) Document your reasons for response when you must resist pressures. Honestly look for alternates.
(7) Have these groups document their requests.
(8) Don't react until you have all the facts, and then don't overreact.
(9) Let individual citizens and organized citizens' groups participate.
(10) Answer a lawyer with a lawyer. Refer any demands made by an attorney, or any requests based upon legal interpretations, to the board of education attorney.

CONSULTANTS

Consultants may be a very valuable resource when properly selected and used by the curriculum improver. The following types of consultants may be used:

– people from other school districts

— state department of education staff members
— people in other local and state governmental agencies
— professors and research specialists from colleges and universities
— staff members of Federal agencies, including the United States Office of Education
— staff members from private foundations
— personnel from private consulting firms
— private individuals

Use of Consultants in the Curriculum Improvement Program

Getting optimum benefit from a consultant or group of consultants is a two-way street. Consultants of national reputation and recognized abilities have often been of little use to a curriculum improvement project because the school district has not planned adequately or wisely for their use.

The following guidelines may help the school district "get its money's worth":

(1) Know what you want them to do—tell them in advance.
(2) Check with a district that has done something similar to what you are doing.
(3) Select consultants that will complement and supplement your staff, not compete with it.
(4) Distinguish between inspirational needs and "roll-up your sleeves" needs—a given project may need both.
(5) Allow the consultant to participate from the beginning.
(6) Study credentials and past performance of private consultants carefully—this is often the most expensive type of service and may not always be the best. Explore other less expensive arrangements.
(7) Clearly establish follow-up procedures expected.
(8) Provide your consultant with background information—not just volumes of district publications but succinct, well-prepared analyses of the problem and his proposed role in its solution.

PROFESSIONAL ORGANIZATIONS

Professional teachers' organizations are demanding and obtaining broader participation in curriculum improvement policies.

These demands vary with the strength and status of such organizations, and may or may not be included as negotiated items in teachers' agreements with boards of education.

The following general guidelines may be of some value depending upon the degree of organization in a particular district. In many cases, agreements already in effect would make these suggestions inoperable:

(1) Allow participation in curriculum discussions even if not required, but do not relinquish your responsibility as the curriculum leader.
(2) Encourage teacher participation in the curriculum improvement process as a normal function outside the professional association structure.
(3) Do not assume that aims of the staff and the association will differ or be irreconcilable. Utilize their demands in obtaining support for desired improvements.
(4) Keep teachers informed, formally and officially, of curriculum improvement plans. Encourage and request their participation.
(5) Use teachers as a channel of communication to assure staff members threatened by innovation.

STATE DEPARTMENT OF EDUCATION

The resources and leadership of state departments of education vary widely from state to state, and within the various departments in a state. However, persons within the state department may provide valuable assistance in the curriculum improvement process. Furthermore, they may have been charged with review, evaluation, and fund approval responsibilities. Always turn to the state department for assistance if it is available, even though you may wish to supplement their services with other assistance.

Guidelines for working with state departments of education are as follows:

(1) Turn to the state department for guidance in any program funded by the state, subject to state review, or based upon state legislation.
(2) Know the ground rules under which state department personnel must work. Mutual understanding of common problems can save embarrassment to all.
(3) Follow the same rules previously given for working with consultants—

know what you want them to do—know what they can provide—send
background information in advance, etc.

(4) Find legitimate reasons to request state department assistance, and
don't overlook such services in favor of the "supersalesman consultant."

(5) Resist the temptation to use the state department as a "whipping
boy."

(6) Become familiar with state department publications—keep channels of
communication open.

(7) Be prompt with required reports.

SUMMARY

It is imperative that the leaders of curriculum improvement
recognize that groups outside the school staff itself must be
informed and should become members of the curriculum improvement team. Furthermore, school systems or schools may not have
enough on-board talent to carry out extensive curriculum improvement projects. In-house capabilities may have to be supplemented
with outside resources and support. Appropriate involvement of
the school board, individual citizens and citizens' groups, and
consultants will make a valuable contribution to planned curriculum improvement.

10

The Systems Approach to Curriculum Improvement

The educational systems approach to curriculum improvement is based upon clearly identified and documented procedures that are designed to facilitate policy-making and decision-making, and to ensure continuing program improvement. The essential elements comprising the educational systems approach are:

(1) Specification of goals and objectives for students of the school or district.
(2) Assessment of the present status of students of the school or district relative to the goals and objectives.
(3) Determination of needs (defined as the discrepancy between the performance of students and the goals and objectives).
(4) Ranking of needs in terms of their priority, and selection of needs for program improvement.
(5) Planning a program that will meet these needs.
(6) Program implementation.
(7) Program evaluation in terms of the extent to which program goals and objectives have been met utilizing the new program.
(8) Continuance, modification, or aborting of the program based upon evaluative findings.

Involvement of administrators, teachers, the school board, public, and students is an inherent aspect of the educational systems approach to curriculum improvement. This chapter deals with:

(1) Determining the value of a systematic procedure for your district or school.
(2) Developing the educational systems approach.
(3) Instituting the educational systems approach.
(4) Decision-making and systematic program improvement.
(5) A basic model for systematic improvement.

DETERMINING THE VALUE OF A SYSTEMATIC PROCEDURE FOR YOUR DISTRICT OR SCHOOL

The educational systems approach is merely a systematic and logical method to facilitate intentional curriculum improvement. It provides a needs-based plan with built-in requirements for evaluation, and extensive involvement of staff time and other resources from the initial planning stages through the total implementation of the program improvement. As noted in Chapter 2, the educational systems approach provides an effective means for making improvements having the following characteristics:

(1) Improvement is of major import and will affect a significant number of teachers, students, and administrators.
(2) Improvement requires extensive cooperation between individuals, departments, and schools.
(3) Improvement has logistic complications.
(4) Improvement is based on identified and documented needs.
(5) Improvement requires significant preplanning and time for development of materials and equipment.
(6) Improvement will be composed of several components.

The systematic approach to educational program improvement is so logical and rational that it is easily accepted for application to educational programs. However, three fundamental errors have been made in applying the model: (1) application of the model to serve goals based upon contradictory values, (2) fragmentation of authority and responsibilities in the application of the model, and (3) lack of clear decision-making procedures.

The invalidity of application of the model to serve goals based on contradictory values becomes evident soon after one begins the curriculum improvement process. Educational systems and schools exist for diverse reasons and often serve conflicting or contradictory goals and objectives. The basic conflicts are those having to do with the values of the various communities and groups served by the schools. Differing values form the foundation for the establishment of specific programs, leaving educational administrators caught in the firing range of conflicting values as expressed in programs demanded by various communities and state laws. Consider the dilemma faced by many school board members and school administrators when bombarded by demands for special programs for handicapped students, gifted students, and economically, culturally, and educationally deprived students.

Fragmentation of authority and responsibility in the application of the model has occurred when the total curriculum improvement process has excluded teachers and program managers from planning, development, and evaluation. The resulting model was such that:

(1) curriculum developers would develop the curriculum,
(2) teachers would teach the curriculum,
(3) students would study the curriculum, and
(4) evaluators would evaluate the curriculum.

The importance of clear decision-making procedures has become increasingly apparent under the present climate for educational decision making where boards of education, citizens' groups, teachers, and students are demanding involvement in determining the curriculum. The educational systems approach provides a vehicle for meaningful involvement of these groups and provides a means for continual communication relative to the status of, and planned improvements in, the curriculum.

From one viewpoint, all curriculum change can be viewed as significant when it affects teachers and students in the classroom. Teachers not involved in the selection of textbooks and instructional materials justifiably may resent the imposition of these materials, thus lessening their effective utilization. Boards of education should not be expected to support curriculum improvement programs if they have not been kept "up-to-speed" relative to the need for the programs and the planning, cost, and expected contribution of the programs to the district's goals and objectives. On the other hand, those charged with curriculum improvement should not be expected to make significant progress if they do not receive support and direction from the school board and key administrator.

DEVELOPING THE EDUCATIONAL SYSTEMS APPROACH

The educational systems approach can be applied at all levels of operation and can meet specific needs for managing curriculum improvement programs within a school district. Chapter 6 discussed the direct involvement of school staffs in planning and implementing curriculum improvement. This is a school-based model that permits and encourages program managers at the classroom, school, supervisory staff, or central office level to determine their own needs, priorities, goals and programs. This approach requires considerable trust and faith on the part of the key administrator in the competencies of staff personnel.

Chapter 11 will approach the curriculum improvement process from the framework of budgeting. A Planning, Programming, Budgeting, Evaluation System (PPBES) will be described that is not only compatible with the school-based systems approach addressed in Chapter 6, but also provides a vehicle for planning district thrusts for improvement by specific program areas (e.g., health services, special education, vocational education.) Chapter 13 presents an evaluation-based curriculum improvement system that views continual and comprehensive evaluative information relative to needs and feasibility, input, process, and product as essential to effective program decision making.

The Educational Systems Team

All educational systems approaches require the establishment of a planning task force to ensure systematic planning, evaluation, and budgeting that will be compatible with goals of the school or district. This planning task force, or educational systems team, will assume many roles and functions as the school or district proceeds through preliminary planning, planning for implementation, program initiation and operation, and evaluation and program improvement. The individual member of the educational systems team will assume more than one role and perform several functions; however, the following capabilities should be represented on the planning team:

— Research and evaluation
— Program development
— Technology and media
— Personnel and staffing
— Finance and budgeting
— Communications and dissemination

Each of these capabilities has been discussed in other sections of this book. Figure 10-1 summarizes the roles and functions of the educational systems team in the curriculum improvement effort.

ROLES AND FUNCTIONS OF THE EDUCATIONAL SYSTEMS TEAM

ROLE	FUNCTION
Research and Evaluation	1. Determination of Program Needs. 2. Development of Program Evaluation Design. 3. Implementation of Evaluation Design 4. Reporting of Evaluative Findings.
Program Development	1. Planning of Program Alternatives that will meet priority needs. 2. Implementation of Approved Program Alternatives.

Figure 10-1

ROLE	FUNCTION
	3. Modification of Programs Based on Evaluative Findings.
	4. Planning for Pilot Implementation, Field Implementation, and Program Adoption.
Technology and Media	1. Determination of Support Requirements for Program Alternatives (Materials, Books, Audio-Visual Equipment, etc.).
	2. Development of Logistical Procedures to Support Program Implementation (Pilot and Field Implementation, or Program Adoption).
	3. Providing Technological and Media Support to Implemented Programs.
Personnel and Staffing	1. Determination of Staffing Requirements for Implementation of Program Alternatives.
	2. Determination of Adequacy of Present Staff for Implementing Program Alternatives.
	3. Determination of Needs for Staff Development or Inservice Requirements to Prepare Staff for Program Implementation.
	4. Staffing for Implementation of Program.
	5. Conducting or Coordinating Staff Development.
Finance and Budgeting	1. Determination of Financial Implications of Planned Program Alternatives (Personnel, Materials, Supplies,

Figure 10-1 (Continued)

ROLE	FUNCTION
	Equipment, Consultants, Communication, Dissemination of Reports, etc.). 2. Determination of Start-Up, Pilot Implementation, Field Implementation, and Program Adoption Costs. 3. Development of Program Budgets. 4. Maintenance of Program Financial Accountability.
Communications and Dissemination	1. Preparation and Dissemination of Program Reports and Documents. 2. Determination of Essential Communications Channels. 3. Development of a Clearing-house for Program-Related Information.

Figure 10-1 (Continued)

Development of a calendar of events will prove to be a valuable planning tool that should be utilized by the educational systems team to ensure coordination of efforts in meeting deadlines for program planning, development, and evaluation. A hypothetical time log, (Figure 10-2) illustrates its use as a road map for the systems team. It should be noted that the development of school or district goals has not been included in this calendar of events.

Development of goals is viewed as too important a task to be relegated to a planning team. Representatives of the board of education, community groups, and the professional staff should be involved in the development of school and district goals. In the case of district goals, the board of education should adopt them as policy so that they can serve as the foundation for all program planning.

EDUCATIONAL SYSTEMS TEAM: CALENDAR OF EVENTS

Phase	Month	Responsibility
Preliminary Planning	June	Develop Needs Assessment Strategy.
	July	Develop Necessary Instruments and Data Gathering Devices.
	August	Finalize Needs Assessment Design.
		Implement Needs Assessment Data Gathering.
	October	Analyze Needs Assessment Data.
		Determine Priority Ranking of Needs.
		Prepare Needs Assessment Report.
	November	Submit Needs Assessment Report to School Board for Review and Approval.
		Submit Needs Assessment Report to Interested Professional and Community Groups.
	December	Obtain Administrative and Board Approval (if necessary) to Plan Program Alternatives that Will Meet Priority Needs.
Planning for Implementation	December	Plan Program Alternatives.
	January	Determine Support, Personnel and Staffing, and Financial Requirements.
	February	Submit Preliminary Program Planning Document to the Key administrator and School

Figure 10-2

EDUCATIONAL SYSTEMS TEAM: CALENDAR OF EVENTS

Phase	Month	Responsibility
Planning for Implementation		Board for Review and Approval.
		Obtain Tentative Commitment of Budget Funds for Program Implementation.
	March	Finalize Program Planning.
	April	Document with Alternative Program Proposals to the Key Administrator and the School Board.
	May	Obtain Commitment to Program Implementation.
		Obtain Program Staff.
	June	Disseminate Program Information to Professional Staff and Media.
	August	Staff Development Activities for Program Staff.
Program Initiation and Operation	September	Implement Program.
		Implement Evaluation Design.

NOTE: This illustrative calendar covers only a 15-month period for planning and initiation of a curriculum improvement program. An entire curriculum improvement cycle would probably take a minimum of three years.

Figure 10-2 (Continued)

INSTITUTING THE EDUCATIONAL SYSTEMS APPROACH

Certain key decision points exist as part of instituting the educational systems approach to curriculum improvement. The first is deciding which type of systems model should be adopted by a district. Among the options for establishing an educational systems approach are the (1) school-based model, (2) the budget-based model, (3) the evaluation-based model, and (4) the central office-based model. Selecting and developing a systems approach for a school district should be based on several considerations. These methods are not mutually exclusive; both the school-based or central office approach will include elements from both the budget model and the evaluative model.

The administrative style of the superintendent or key administrator is probably the most important variable in determining what approach to take in systematic program planning. Does the key administrator encourage initiative on the part of teachers, principals, and others, and does he trust their judgment and have faith that their plans for program improvement are based on priority needs? If so, the school-based systems planning model as discussed in Chapter 6 can be implemented; if not, a systematic approach that maintains direction and control at the level of the key administrator should be implemented.

The research, program development, and evaluation capacity of the district can provide the necessary framework for establishing the educational systems approach. Does the district have a research, program development, and evaluation capacity at the level of the key administrator, or does the district possess the necessary talent to create such a capacity? If it does, the evaluation-based model discussed in Chapter 13 can be implemented; if it does not, the necessary talent will have to be secured or a school-based model for improvement will have to be implemented.

The financial planning process within the district provides a vehicle for implementing a systematic approach to curriculum improvement. Does the district encourage budget preparation by individual program managers as described in Chapter 11, or does the superintendent maintain control of all budget considerations including program improvement thrusts? If the district permits program manager budget input, the procedures as described in Chapter 11 may be quite appropriate; if not, a central staff or task force-based approach to program budgeting will be more appropriate.

The availability of comprehensive information relative to program strengths, deficiencies, and omissions will assist the district in moving directly into a systematic program improvement effort. Does the district possess comprehensive information relative to the status of the district's programs in terms of the needs of the student population? If data are available and indicate that common program deficiencies or omissions exist across the district, then the district should develop a central staff-based approach to dealing with these deficiencies and omissions. If such data are not available, a task force-based system should be created to conduct needs and feasibility studies.

DECISION-MAKING AND SYSTEMATIC PROGRAM IMPROVEMENT

Once the decision to implement a systematic procedure for curriculum improvement has been made, the board of education and the key administrator must play essential roles in implementing the procedure. The board of education, charged by the public with establishing policies for the school district and overseeing the educational enterprise, participates in the curriculum improvement program by making decisions relative to program support in terms of allocated personnel, materials, and dollars. The key administrator, as the executive officer of the board, has the responsibility for bringing matters before the board for action. Whether or not the key administrator is directly involved in the curriculum improvement effort as part of the educational systems team, he is responsible for providing clear direction for those involved. Attempts to implement a new program without clear direction and support will flounder.

Guidelines for Decision-Making

Establishment of procedures and guidelines will facilitate decision-making by the key administrator and the board of education, and provide stability to the curriculum improvement effort. The following procedural elements are unique to the planning and implementation of new programs, and understanding and acceptance of them will facilitate wise decision making.

(1) Program plans, implementation plans, and program reports detailing short- and long-range implications should be submitted in writing to the key administrator and board of education prior to requests for approval and support.

(2) Systematic curriculum improvement will usually require one year for preliminary planning and program development; one year for program implementation and operation on a limited or pilot study basis; and one year for expanded or field study program implementation. In some instances, a program may be adopted across a school district during the third year of the curriculum improvement effort.

(3) Program evaluation reports may be out-of-phase with the district's budgeting calendar. Commitments to funding for the ensuing year's activities are essential for continued program development and implementation.

(4) Modifications of operational programs may be necessary throughout the pilot and field study, but these modifications should be well justified and documented.

(5) Program costs for implementing and operating a new program usually will be greater than the cost for operating a regular program.

Many school districts have adopted policies governing the procedures to be followed in the decision-making process. The establishment of such policies facilitates decision-making and provides direction to the key administrator and his staff. A recommended procedure is that items for school board action be introduced as informational items at least one meeting (or one month) prior to their expected approval. Such a procedure permits the board of education to request additional information, and provides the key administrator with ample time to prepare that information.

Systematic educational planning can be viewed as educational decision making where each step in the process consists of developing proposals that can and must be responded to with approval or disapproval. Significant yes/no decision points that are inherent in the planning and implementation of curriculum improvements include:

(1) Shall we institute an educational systems approach?
(2) Shall we accept the findings of the needs assessment study?
(3) Do we agree with the priority listing of program needs?

(4) Shall we support the development of program alternatives designed to meet the priority needs?

(5) Which program alternative(s) do we wish to see developed further?

(6) Shall we accept the program development proposal for implementation:

  (a) Pilot test, field test, or program adoption?
  (b) Adequacy of program design?
  (c) Adequacy of media and technology support?
  (d) Adequacy of personnel to implement the program?
  (e) Adequacy of staff development program?
  (f) Adequacy and appropriateness of the evaluation design?
  (g) Financial feasibility of program implementation?
  (h) Adequacy of procedures for communication and dissemination?

(7) Shall we approve program funding for 1, 2, or 3 years (contingent upon program evaluation findings)?

(8) Shall we accept the program evaluation report?

(9) Should the program be modified, expanded, or curtailed?

A BASIC MODEL FOR SYSTEMATIC IMPROVEMENT

A basic model illustrating the essential elements comprising the systematic curriculum improvement procedure follows.[1] This model conceptualizes the planning, management, decision-making, and evaluation phases of program improvement described in this chapter and in Chapters 6, 11, and 13; and represents a cycle of activities extending through the period of time needed to accommodate a specific program. (See Figure 10-3.)

In examining the model, the reader will find three planes or levels. The top line represents a feedback and recycling potential which is not limited to any single phase but moves from each phase to its previous phase, *as necessary*. The row of numbered blocks indicates a program's various phases. The third row of symbols indicates program evaluation, which is a continuous process. The solid lines of the model show direct flows of information and/or relatedness; the broken lines show a less direct relationship.

---

[1] Adapted from: Tennant, W. Jack and Charles L. Bertram *Planning for Educational Change: PPBS,* Center for Effecting Educational Change, Fairfax County Public Schools, Fairfax, Virginia, July 1969.

A BASIC MODEL FOR SYSTEMATIC IMPROVEMENT

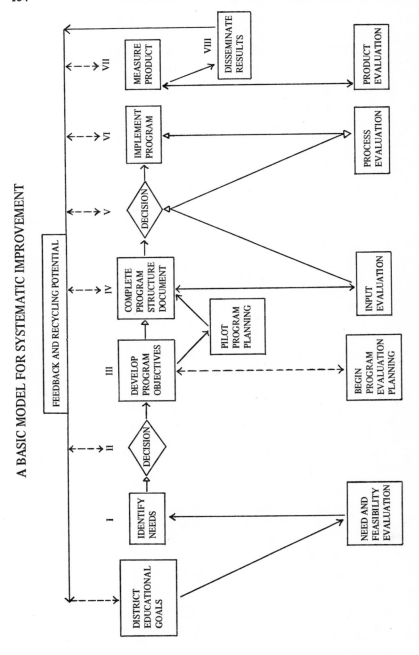

Figure 10-3

The model's overall function is to trace the problem-solving procedure and is not intended to be static at any point or phase. The feedback and recycling potential is designed to allow continuous revision and analysis during the program's development. To illustrate, if it were decided that an objective should be expanded to include other closely related objectives or needs, the feedback could move from Block III, effecting the recycling of all products from the objective phase back to the need and feasibility evaluation phase. At that point, an analysis could be made of the original evaluation of need and feasibility, and data concerning the other closely related objectives could be fed into the original evaluation to create an expanded objective and new priority.

Several points should be emphasized in connection with the model. First, it is not intended to constitute a rigid guideline from which no departure can be made. It is meant, instead, to be altered for various circumstances and needs. Second, although it calls for evaluation of all output, the evaluation need not be only objective or statistical in nature. All output in education cannot be quantified and no attempt should be made to do so. Finally, the step-by-step procedure, as outlined, produces detailed and comprehensive data. If these data are to be efficiently and productively used, they must be organized, analyzed, and stored for the ready accessibility of decision makers.

This chapter has dealt with determining the value of a systematic procedure for your district or school, developing the educational systems approach, the educational systems team, instituting the educational systems approach, decision making and systematic program improvement, and a basic model for systematic improvement. Additional information on the school-based model, budget-based model, and evaluation-based model is contained in Chapters 6, 11, and 13 respectively.

11

Financing Curriculum Improvement

The school administrator's task as a curriculum innovator is becoming increasingly difficult. Proponents of accountability are concerned with the rising costs of providing the basic education program for children and with the increasing costs of salaries, fringe benefits, and instructional materials which have driven the cost of education to all time highs. Boards of education, community organizations, and parents are taking a second look at rising costs and questioning whether they are getting their money's worth. Within this climate, curriculum improvement programs with high price tags will have a limited chance of implementation. Innovations of the type that can be implemented with small or no increases in the school system's budget stand a better chance for approval.

School systems will always have needs that can be satisfied through some type of curriculum improvement. Within the limited financial resources of a school district, meeting identified needs becomes difficult and invariably results in the establishment of priorities. Developing a priority list of needs is an essential task in the effective management of financial resources.

Another important task that coincides with developing priority lists of needs for curriculum improvement is the necessity for the school administrator to analyze current practices in the district. He should not make the mistake of assuming that what is currently being done in his district cannot be done better and at less cost. Funds saved from curtailing or eliminating certain programs can be used to implement or improve others. This type of financing can be thought of as "program tradeoffs." The school administrator must be willing to consider "tradeoffs" as a viable alternative to funding new curriculum improvement programs.

If viable tradeoffs do not exist, the new curriculum improvement plan will cost additional dollars. Care must be exercised in stating the plan in terms of desired outcomes and with specific cost estimates for implementing the plan. The objectives or desired outcomes of the plan should be stated in measurable terms and should include both objective and subjective criteria for measurement.

A new curriculum improvement plan designed to meet some identified need should include alternative action plans. For example, one alternative plan may cost thousands of dollars less than the curriculum improvement plan recommended yet come very close to fully meeting the district's need. This type of planning will give the board of education additional information concerning the nature, scope, and possible ways to meet the program need. Also a curriculum improvement plan should include both short- and long-range revenue and expenditure estimates. A one- or two-year plan is considered short-range while long-range estimates should project five years into the future.

CURRICULUM IMPROVEMENT CYCLE

The curriculum improvement cycle outlined in Chapter 3 contained four major steps:

(1) Preliminary planning
(2) Planning for implementation
(3) Initiation and operation
(4) Evaluation and program improvement

Each of these steps has a specific relationship to financing a curriculum improvement program. It is imperative that the administrator key these steps to his unique budget circumstances. This usually involves coordinating the planning for new programs with the budgeting process in the school district.

Preliminary Planning

The preliminary planning stage is crucial in getting a new program "off the ground." It involves obtaining the financial commitment of the district to additional funds for curriculum improvement or determining what program tradeoffs can be made to provide the needed financial resources. At this stage, estimates of revenues and expenditures should be made for the project and submitted to the board of education for approval. The budget document serves as the vehicle for communicating to the board and public the funding requirements of the proposed plan.

The budget document should include estimates of all line item expenditures; e.g. funds budgeted for teacher salaries, equipment, travel, etc., and the revenue to support the project. More will be said about this stage later in this chapter.

Planning for Implementation

Planning for implementation of a project is the second stage of the curriculum improvement cycle. At this stage a document containing implementation and evaluation plans should be prepared. The detailed budget prepared in the preliminary planning stage should be included and be compatible with the accounting procedures of the district. In the event that an outside agency (Federal, state, or local) is funding the project, the accounting procedures used must also meet the requirements of that agency. Realizing that the budget detail contains estimates of expenditures and revenues, it is necessary to establish the amount of flexibility the program manager has in transferring funds from one account to another. For example, after several months of operation, project needs may vary from those originally estimated. More supplies may be needed, while the amount of equipment needed was overestimated. The policy framework required to make these kinds of decisions should be made during this stage of the curriculum improvement cycle.

Initiation and Operation

The financial implications of initiating and operating the project involve conforming to the accounting guidelines developed in the planning stage. Periodic review of the financial reports of the project is necessary to ensure that funding levels will not be exceeded. Many districts have accounting systems that provide program managers with monthly or quarterly statements of revenue received, revenue balance due, funds disbursed, funds committed but not spent, and uncommitted balances for each line item of the budget. Districts not providing this type of information should develop such systems as soon as possible. These financial data are essential for the estimating of revenues and expenditures throughout the project and help ensure that the project is in control financially.

Evaluation and Improvement

The last stage in the curriculum improvement process is evaluation of the project. From a financial point of view, this involves comparing actual costs with estimated costs and relating these costs to benefits of the project. (See Chapter 13 on techniques to be used in determining program benefits.) It is also necessary to prepare the accounting records for an audit. This involves the process of reviewing the records to ensure that there are no outstanding receivables or liabilities for the project. Usually this task can be performed by the staff or the school district's business office.

CURRICULUM IMPROVEMENT AND THE BUDGET PROCESS

The curriculum improvement process must coincide with the budget process if it is to be successful. A nationwide thrust is evident in establishing management decision-making systems that force an amalgamation of these processes. Terms such as MBO

(Management by Objectives) and PPBES (Planning, Programing, Budgeting, Evaluation System) are now familiar terms to the school administrator. Growing out of private enterprise, these management systems have given educators a valuable tool for ensuring that decisions affecting educational programs are made with the best available information.

PPBES has probably gained the widest acceptance as a management tool for educators. In fact, some states have mandated that their school districts implement some form of PPBES. As a process, PPBES has several key steps which the school administrator can use in developing curriculum improvement programs. These steps are:

(1) Identification of needs to be met and putting them in order of priority.
(2) Development of objectives to meet priority needs.
(3) Design of plans and alternatives to achieve objectives.
(4) Development of cost estimates for all plans on short- and long-term bases.
(5) Implementation of the plan that best meets the educational needs of the district within its financial resources.
(6) Evaluation of results of the program using objective and subjective criteria.
(7) If results are unsatisfactory, analysis of objectives, plans, and evaluative criteria of the present program to ensure that future changes in the program satisfy district needs.

Whatever management system the school administrator chooses to use in effecting curriculum improvement, the key ingredients are the identified needs of the district and the objectives developed to meet the needs.

Within this context, the budget document is a valuable tool for the school administrator interested in curriculum improvement. It can communicate the need for curriculum improvement to the board of education and school patrons in the district. Also, it puts the program need into the context of the total school district's needs and programs. The need for a new curriculum improvement program is forced to compete with current programs for a share of the funds. This is a healthy environment for the school administrator in that it requires him to prepare extensive justification for the funding of new programs if they are to be approved by the board and taxpayers.

In the past, the budget document has served as the primary vehicle for communicating the cost of educational programs to the board of education and taxpayers. To the school administrator interested in implementing a new program, the budget document must serve a broader purpose. It must reflect program objectives and program plans in addition to program costs. Anything short of this information may reduce the chances for approval of funds to support a new program.

Many school districts are moving toward the formulation of budgets on a "program" basis. This is consistent with the application of PPBES as an educational management system. The program budget provides costs of educational programs; e.g., the cost of the kindergarten program, student activities program, or reading program. On the other hand, the traditional "line item" budget provided costs on a line item basis; e.g., the cost of teacher salaries, instructional aide salaries, utilities, or supplies.

The program budget also provides for long-range cost estimates for implementing programs. In addition to cost data on school district programs, the program budget should include the following kinds of information:

- program objectives, i.e., definitive statements of the proposed outcomes of the program for a given period of time
- implementation plans for programs to ensure that objectives are met
- alternative strategies for achieving the proposed outcomes of the program
- evaluative information on past performance of programs including objective as well as subjective data

The school administrator can use the program budget to his advantage. Advantages of a program budget include:

- it permits the cost of the curriculum improvement program to be segregated from other costs in the budget
- it can serve as a program as well as financial document to the school administrator
- if the need exists, the program budget usually permits the reallocation of funds within the total program
- if developed properly, the program budget forces the board of education to look at the cost versus projected benefit of programs prior to making decisions

— since long-range cost estimates are included, the program budget
strengthens the chances for a long-term commitment of funds to a new
program provided the program operates successfully

FINANCIAL PLANNING FOR CURRICULUM IMPROVEMENT

The preliminary planning stage of the curriculum improvement
cycle is crucial in getting a new program "off the ground." It is at
this stage that the major portion of the financial planning for the
new program must be completed.

The financial plan for a new program involves completion of
several key tasks. They include:

(1) development of estimates of expenditures by line item for the new
program (projected for five years).
(2) determination of sources of revenue to support the new program for a
five year period.
(3) development of alternative programs with reduced resources that will
meet the program need to a lesser extent.
(4) pulling all of the above information together into a program budget
including narratives outlining program objectives, program plans, and
program performance indicators. This becomes part of the preliminary
planning document discussed on page 43.
(5) ensuring that all plans for the new program coincide with the school
district's budget process.

Good financial planning implies that these tasks will be done
prior to planning for implementation of the new program. However, to complete these tasks, program objectives and plans must
be completed. The planning cycle dictates that program objectives
must be formulated prior to developing plans to achieve the
objectives, and program plans must be completed prior to making
cost estimates for the program.

Each of the five tasks just outlined should be approached in a
systematic way to ensure that all facets of the program are
covered. Some hints that may assist the school administrator in
completing these tasks follow. Examples of forms to gather and
present the program and financial data are given also.

Estimating Personnel Costs

Estimating personnel costs is the most important area to consider in estimating program costs since approximately 80 percent of the total program costs will be in the personnel category. Sufficient time should be spent in making estimates of personnel costs. In estimating costs for new personnel positions, determination of the following factors will facilitate accurate estimates:

(1) the number and types of positions needed
(2) the qualifications for employment; e.g., previous experience, certification, advanced degrees
(3) the length of contract for each type of position
(4) what fringe benefits are available for new personnel; e.g., retirement, group health coverage, the number of sick and/or annual leave days permitted without loss of pay

Using school district salary schedules and the preceding information, cost estimates for each position can be made. Caution should be exercised in determining salary costs for future years where salary schedules do not exist. (The best method for approximating future salary costs is to take the average yearly salary scale increase and apply it to the current scale for each of the five years needed for the five-year financial plan.)

Where cost of living increases in salaries and fringe benefits are provided by the school district, use the same source document to determine the cost-of-living increase (e.g., the monthly report of the U.S. Bureau of Labor and Statistics), and apply the average for two or three years to the current scale for each of the five successive years. (This same technique should be used in estimating costs for equipment, instructional materials, etc., to adjust for inflation.) Other personnel costs which may be incurred include substitute teacher pay, overtime pay, consultant fees, and part-time employees pay.

Estimating Other Costs

Other program requirements which may add additional costs to the new program include: office equipment for personnel and media equipment for instructional uses; office supplies, printing, postage, and instructional materials including textbooks, library books, audio-visual materials, etc.; travel funds for personnel; and minor building modifications such as removing permanent classroom walls to provide open space for instructional purposes.

Estimates of these costs can be made accurately if the proper research is done. For example, equipment and supply costs can be estimated utilizing manufacturers' or distributors' catalogs. Labor and material costs for a building modification can be estimated utilizing figures from an independent contractor if the project cannot be handled by school district employees. Otherwise, material costs for building modifications can be made by school district employees.

Estimating Revenue

Revenue to fund a new program usually is derived from a categorical grant from a Federal, state, or local agency, or from the local school district's tax revenues. If a categorical grant is being requested, it usually requires some local district financial support—either direct funding of certain items in the budget proposal or indirect support of the program through the use of certain school district services. This type of indirect support is commonly referred to as "in kind" support. With respect to a categorical grant program, the school administrator would be wise to request the board of education to set aside contingency funds in the event the grant program is discontinued prior to its planned expiration date. This would preclude the loss of valuable data on the performance of the program prior to its completion.

Alternative Programs

Faced with meeting an identified need, the school administrator plans a curriculum improvement and projects financial resources to support a program that best meets the need of the school district. However, it is a fact that many excellent program plans cannot be implemented because of insufficient funds. It is also a fact that many excellent program plans can be implemented at reduced funding levels and still accomplish most of what the original program was designed to accomplish. The key issue for the administrator to consider is the preparation of alternative program plans with reduced funding levels. For example, if a curriculum improvement plan is estimated to cost $100,000, what portions of the plan can be implemented with a 10, 15, or 20 percent reduction in funding? Further, will these alternative plans meet the district's need to some worthwhile extent? Good preliminary planning requires consideration of these types of alternatives.

The Program Budget

The program budget for a curriculum improvement proposal should pull together narrative information (including objectives, short- and long-range plans, and performance criteria) and financial data into one document to be presented to the board of education. Figures 11-1 and 11-2 provide illustrations of how a large suburban school system presents this information. With this information, the board will know what, when, and how much it is getting from a proposal and how much the proposal will cost.

The Budget Process

Most school districts operate on an annual funding basis with the fiscal year established for a twelve-month period, usually July 1 to June 30, or January 1 to December 31. The calendar for preparation and implementation of a budget for a given fiscal year should begin from nine to twelve months prior to the beginning of the fiscal year. This is necessary to ensure that decisions on educational programs are made in time to allow for the program to "gear-up." An example of a budget calendar used in a large suburban school system is shown in Figure 11-3. Note the number of levels where decisions are required on a program proposal. These levels of decision-making will vary depending upon the organizational structure of the school system and whether it is fiscally independent or fiscally dependent.

THE PLAN FOR IMPROVEMENT
YEAR
_____HIGH SCHOOL

ACCOUNTABILITY STATEMENT

[Information should be presented here which will report on the progress of currently operating programs. Also, where program needs exist, objective and subjective data should be given as evidence that a need exists.]

PROGRAM OBJECTIVES

[The objectives to be accomplished if the new program is implemented should be stated. They should be stated in measurable terms with a time-frame for achievement given. Short- and long-term objectives should be highlighted.]

PROGRAM PLANS

[Short- and long-range plans designed to meet the objectives should be given. This would include statements of overall techniques to be used; e.g., open spaced classrooms with teachers and paraprofessionals will work on an individual basis with children; continuous progress will be permitted with course credit awarded when program objectives are achieved by the student.]

PROGRAM PERFORMANCE INDICATORS

[The evaluation scheme to be used in judging the degree of attainment of objectives is stated here. If statistical data are employed, pre- and post-data should be given. Subjective criteria should indicate who will make the judgment and that a comparison of that judgment will be made with baseline information.]

ALTERNATIVE PLANS

[Using the plan for improvement as a baseline, outline here what objectives and plans will have to be postponed if a reduced funding level is approved.]

Figure 11-1

THE BUDGET PLAN

YEAR
_____ HIGH SCHOOL

REVENUE	FY_____ (Estimate for first year)	FY_____ (Estimate for second year)	FY_____ (Estimate for third year)	ALTERNATIVES FOR FY _____	
				10% Reduction	20% Reduction
Categorical					
Federal					
State					
Local					
Noncategorical					
Federal					
State					
Local					
Tuition					
Other	_____	_____	_____	_____	_____
Total					
EXPENDITURES					
Personnel					
Teachers					
Aides					
Part time					
Other					
Equipment					
Supplies					
Travel					
Other	_____	_____	_____	_____	_____
Total					

Figure 11-2

THE BUDGET CALENDAR YEAR

May–August   Preliminary planning by program manager with teachers, students, and community. Program needs, objectives, plans, costs, etc., identified.

Figure 11-3

THE BUDGET CALENDAR YEAR

September	Program managers (principals and other department heads) submit to appropriate superior:
	1. *Plan for Improvement*
	2. *Budget Plan* including long-range estimates
	3. *Plan for Improvement* and *Budget Plan* with a 10% and 20% reduction in funding
September	Public hearing.
October	Approved program plans and budgets submitted to Superintendent for consideration.
November	Publish total school system budget including *Plans for Improvement* and *Budget Plans* submitted by program manager and approved by Superintendent.
December	Public hearing.
January	Board of Education budget hearings.
April	Approval of Budget by Board of Education and advertisement of tax rates to support it. (This assumes fiscal independence of the school district. If the school district is fiscally dependent, another decision level is added to the calendar.)
May—June	Completion of planning for program implementation.
July	Program initiation.

Figure 11-3 (Continued)

12

Instructional Materials, Facilities, and Equipment in Curriculum Improvement

Planned programs for curriculum improvement generally encounter the costly world of instructional materials, facilities, and equipment. Most administrators will agree that the selection and effective use of materials, facilities, and equipment are essential factors in improving the learning process. It follows that any systematic program for curriculum change and improvement must incorporate methods and procedures for selection and effective utilization. You must know what is needed; how, when, and where it can be obtained; what training or orientation is required before it can be used effectively; and what can be expected in terms of results. Many administrators find that such information is not readily available when decisions concerning the purchase of materials, facilities, and equipment are required. This condition often prevails in school system environments where funds are programmed rather than seeking funding for needed programs; where instructional programs are forced to fit available facilities rather than designing facilities to accommodate instructional programs; and where expensive technological systems such as computers or television are purchased without knowing their effectiveness in terms of specific needs or how to use them

169

properly. In this chapter, the administrator will find suggestions, sources of information, and alternative procedures for planning, selecting, and evaluating instructional materials, facilities, and equipment.

INSTRUCTIONAL MATERIALS

In many school districts, supervisors and administrators select materials on the basis of a review of the curriculum and the knowledge of the individual supervisor of what materials are available in the educational marketplace. In some systems they may be catalogued and distributed like library books, placed on shelves, and checked out to teachers. The evaluation of these materials may be based upon frequency of use or rates of consumption instead of their effectiveness in contributing to the attainment of instructional objectives.

Programs to change and improve the curriculum often encounter problems of inflexibility and nonresponsiveness under systems where the selection and distribution of materials are left to the judgment and experience of departmental or curriculum area supervisors. If the origination of new programs to change and improve the curriculum is desired and encouraged at all levels within the system, a new role must be assumed by the key administrator. He must:

(1) Ensure that materials are selected and procured on a need basis.
(2) Institute procedures to provide them when and where they are needed.
(3) Provide training for users in their use if required.
(4) Ensure that materials are evaluated in terms of program objectives.
(5) Disseminate information on the availability and effectiveness of materials.

The need for the services and support listed here is common to instructional systems of any size ranging from a team of teachers to a large school district. Unless they are available, administrators responsible for improving instructional programs will continue to face item-by-item decisions regarding the purchase and utilization of materials without the necessary information concerning need and effectiveness. The school administrator should always provide these services as part of any curriculum improvement program.

Selection and Utilization Based Upon Needs

Any system for selecting and utilizing instructional materials based upon needs must have two major components:

(1) Inclusion of material and resource selection in the entire planning process.
(2) Methods and procedures for determining needs and making selections.

In the first instance, requirements for such materials and the resources necessary to provide them must be a part of the planning of programs to change and improve instruction. The program plan might include a pilot and field test phase, continuous documentation, the design and use of inservice packages, testing and evaluation, and dissemination, all of which might generate requirements for instructional materials. Too many program proposals consist chiefly of additional personnel spaces without adequate provision for materials and necessary inservice activities. Unless requirements are included in the planning, and resources provided for fulfilling these requirements at the time of program submission and approval, the key administrator will find serious problems in obtaining the funding support and cooperation necessary to carry out the program.

Secondly, there must be methods and procedures for generating needs for instructional materials from the instructional program level. This implies that any participant in the effort to achieve specified program objectives may provide a contribution to the identification and selection of appropriate materials. These participants include both teachers and learners, as well as program managers, consultants, parents, and those supervisors and administrators involved in the program. The starting point should be the teacher in her role as instructional resource manager for her class. Material needs can be defined from reviewing the plan or strategy to be followed to achieve her instructional objectives.

For example, a plan might require the following steps for a unit in Social Studies:

(1) Introduce subject area.
(2) Learning of certain facts and background information.
(3) Small group or individual study and research.
(4) Student presentation of findings for discussion.
(5) Summary of what has been learned.
(6) Evaluation (Have instructional objectives been achieved?).

Using a simple worksheet as illustrated in Figure 12-1 the teacher can set forth her materials requirements in terms of what she hopes they will accomplish, and begin to identify specific materials in terms of her own experience.

This process, as illustrated, is repeated for each of the elements of the plan or strategy for the instructional program. The teacher may turn to other teachers, media and materials specialists, or supervisors and administrators for suggestions on items to fulfill the materials requirements for each step of the plan. The worksheet will also provide the basis for assessment of the effectiveness of items of instructional materials in terms of fulfilling specific requirements.

Subject area specialists, consultants, or the nature and design of the instructional program involved may generate materials requirements, and in some cases call for specific items to achieve program objectives. For example, instructional materials may be incorporated into diagnostic and skill development functions of early childhood or special education programs. Research and evaluation data may indicate that certain materials can best achieve certain results thus meeting the needs of handicapped or very young children.

SAMPLE WORKSHEET FOR DETERMINING MATERIAL NEEDS FOR SOCIAL STUDIES

Activity	Materials Requirements	Items Suggested
1. Introduction	Stimulate interest, curiosity, involvement in subject. Available for	Kit B-432 (on hand) Life Magazine 6/36 Marine Compass

Figure 12-1

Activity	Materials Requirements	Items Suggested
	placement in classroom before unit begins. Visual items for board, realia (significance unknown if possible). Evidence of controversy about subject area personalities or events.	Sextant Copies of newspaper extracts of June 36 Reprint of Congressional record of 12 June, 1936.
2. Background Information	Provide all students with a common understanding of the history and development of the subject area, key issues and problems, and pertinent references.	

Figure 12-1 (Continued)

Programs such as the Elementary Science Studies (ESS) program rely on specific packages of materials as essential to the conduct of the activity. Caution is in order when specific materials are considered mandatory, and imposed without alternatives upon teachers by program administrators, supervisors, or specialists. This practice ignores individual characteristics and learning patterns of students, teacher strengths and weaknesses, and environmental variables and seems only justifiable when highly structured, specialized, or standardized programs are desired.

Distribution Procedures

Programs to change and improve the curriculum will often require special procedures to ensure that instructional materials are provided when and where they are needed. Existing materials distribution systems may not be flexible enough to meet these needs due to lead time requirements, delivery schedules, or availability restrictions. Such systems often operate according to experience data and, in a sense, are designed and stocked to meet last year's needs. New programs may present new and different distribution and storage patterns due to requirements for extensive staff development, demonstrations, and materials evaluation activities. If the instructional materials are selected on a need basis and are essential to achieving program objectives, then they must enjoy special priorities and handling if they are to be available on time in the right place.

These problems may be solved by using one or more of the following methods:

(1) Provide for use and distribution priorities in your program planning at the same time you provide the resources for the materials. Approval of the program will also constitute a requirement upon the materials distribution system in your district to observe these priorities.

(2) Place all materials necessary for the development of your program under the control of the program manager. He may have to operate and control a distribution system independent of any existing procedures.

(3) Establish one or more material centers. These facilities would be available for staff development, demonstrations, field testing, and also serve as distribution points.

(4) Publish a materials handbook listing all special materials for the program, what they should accomplish in terms of instructional objectives, and how to get them.

Staff Development

New programs often involve new materials or new uses and applications of existing materials. Both require that users receive training in the proper use of selected materials. This process cannot be left to chance or later action. It must be included in the planning of the program, and resources provided for this purpose. Staff development in the uses of instructional materials may include demonstrations by distributors or consultants, video-tapes or films of the materials being used under actual classroom conditions, and practice with children under the observation and guidance of specialists or instructors.

Program planning and approval must allow sufficient lead time to ensure that materials are on hand and available for initial staff development activities related to the program effort. Procurement and delivery priorities may be required if your school system has established procedures that call for the ordering of materials on a seasonal schedule.

A training handbook describing effective ways to use program materials should be developed and widely distributed. This document will prove valuable for orienting new teachers or school staffs. The preparation of the handbook can be incorporated into your staff development program and field testing. Specialists and experienced teachers can provide most of the content if they are assigned this responsibility as a part of their involvement in the program.

Video-tapes and audio-tapes of the training program can also be prepared and will prove useful for training new teachers or for subsequent staff development workshops.

Materials Evaluation

Instructional materials should be evaluated only in terms of what they accomplish and how they are used. They have little intrinsic value. The proper response to the question, "How good is this film?" or "How good is *Sesame Street*?" should be "For what?" We need to know the purpose of using any instructional material before we can assess its worth, but ignoring this is a common error committed by school districts in their attempts to evaluate their often costly programs for instructional materials. Many methods are employed including preview and review panels, assessments by enterprises and institutions such as the Educational Film Library (EFL) brochures of program distributors, and analyses of frequency of use data (based on the questionable assumption that if many people use something many times it must be good).

Provision should be made for the evaluation of instructional materials in the program plan. This should be a major part of the pilot or field test phase of a curriculum improvement effort because it is safe to assume that we can determine which items are more effective in achieving desired results more economically in a small program than in a program for the entire school district. A simple evaluation plan might consist of the following elements:

(1) Materials effectiveness in terms of pupil achievement as revealed by pre- and post-measures adopted to measure overall program effectiveness.

(2) Materials effectiveness in terms of teacher assessment of their worth in achievement of instructional goals.

(3) Materials effectiveness in terms of pupil interest and involvement as revealed by classroom observation and teacher reaction.

(4) Materials design assessment in terms of cost, durability, maintenance (if appropriate), and consumption rates, as revealed by field testing.

Materials evaluation procedures must be continuous if they are to be effective. This means documentation by teachers of the use of each item and its effectiveness as it is used in the program. We cannot rely on memory after the program is completed. Records must include details on how materials were used as well as what materials were used. These records will provide the basis for interpreting significant results, good or bad, in the overall program evaluation, and enable the evaluator to identify and pass on to other users what materials can be most effectively used, and how they can be most effectively used to achieve specific objectives.

Dissemination

The results of planning for instructional materials on a need basis, experiences with these materials during staff development and field testing, and what is learned about them from our evaluation should be made available to future program participants and to the school community. The major document for this purpose should be some sort of program evaluation report which can be completed at the end of the pilot or field testing phase, preferably before the program is adopted or rejected. The report should include a section or supplement devoted to the materials utilized, grouped according to the instructional objectives they relate to. Information describing how they were used and how effective they were in achieving the objective, as well as the source of the assessment, is needed. The report may include a recommended package of the most effective materials and be designed to provide a feasible basis for funding and implementing the program.

Other dissemination materials include handbooks listing materials, their effectiveness, how to get them, and, perhaps, a handbook for teachers describing how to use them most effectively to achieve specific instructional goals. Materials should be updated as experience in the program increases. New and better items will appear on the market and the staff should continually develop more effective techniques, not resting on its laurels once the program is implemented. Dissemination, like evaluation, must be continuous and should be a part of operational as well as developmental programs if we are to keep pace with the changing needs of students.

FACILITIES

No decisions required of the school administrator are quite as costly, quite as visible, or more lasting, sometimes embarrassingly so, than those involved in school construction and modification. Few districts conduct meaningful long-range planning that includes instructional programs spelling out what facilities will be required in the near and distant future. Most educators agree that facilities play a significant role in the learning process, but most are willing to accept whatever the current environment has to offer. Those with new schools are fortunate. Those who must cope with older and less comfortable schools must wait and do the best they can with what they have. Only the larger districts enjoy the services of school construction specialists with the capability of working hand-in-hand with instructional planners to ensure that school construction and modification is planned to meet present and future instructional needs. Smaller systems may require consultants or work with state-based construction personnel and architects.

The construction of new facilities or significant modification of old facilities should be based upon need in the same manner as the acquisition of materials. There will be few instances when you can design a facility for a particular program for curriculum improvement and then move in and implement your innovation. However, the evaluation of existing facilities in terms of providing or not providing optimum environments for new programs should be planned and carried out in the same manner as programs are evaluated. This information can provide the basis for facility specifications when you have the opportunity to build new structures or modify old ones.

Modern construction and modification alternatives offer a flexibility that was not available in earlier designs by providing open spaces, movable walls and partitions, and small and large group learning pods and areas that may serve a host of activities and subjects. If the long-range planning of the district is not "locked in" to a particular strategy or simply does not exist, this type of flexible construction may be desirable. Remember the facility that is built or modified will be with the district for a long time into the future. Develop plans on the basis of what can be learned about current program needs, but build in the flexibility to meet future needs as well. Current needs can be formulated from evaluation of the strengths and weaknesses of existing facilities, what alternatives exist without construction or modification (improvisation, adaptation, self-production), and consideration of construction or significant modification based on specifications derived from the preceding process. Designs should be chosen from existing plans if possible. Visiting similar facilities can be particularly important if there is a district with experience in implementing similar instructional programs or philosophies. The high cost of school construction or modification justifies detailed and careful planning, as well as the spending of travel or consultant funds, to make sure that the district does not make costly errors or end up with unsuitable facilities.

EQUIPMENT SYSTEMS

Many budgets for major curriculum improvement programs contain healthy amounts of dollars for technological systems such as television and computers without the understanding, experience, and training necessary to use them effectively, or even an idea of what instructional needs they can best meet. The administrator faced with making decisions about such systems will encounter a host of sales representatives promoting educational systems hardware and software directly to the educational community. During the early days of Title III, many corporations formed educational departments and affiliates and a large number of new companies were founded in the environment of Federal funding. Consultants flourished. The local school superintendent and his staff became fair game as they walked down the display aisles at the annual conventions. Sales representatives offered expensive technological system packages complete with proposal and specification writing services to facilitate outside funding assistance. Aside from the lack of knowledge and purpose to use such systems effectively, many school systems found themselves with costly maintenance and replacement problems when the funding ran out. As school administrators today, we face increasing demands for accountability in an environment of the rising costs of running our schools and rising community resistance to higher taxes. Equipment systems are often the first casualties in such trends. Equipment systems that cannot prove their effectiveness, or that are used far below capacity, will surely be most vulnerable.

But all modern school systems seem to have television and computers, don't they? Our journals are full of pictures of children at study carrels with headsets, viewscreens, and terminal keyboards, or grouped around the television receiver in the corner of the classroom. Modern school buildings are designed for such systems and many critics calling for the modernization of our schools envision the future classroom as a learning resource center resplendent with teaching machines serving the individual needs of children. So how do you decide what and how much to buy when it all costs too much? So many different systems are offered; some sources predict that what you want will soon be obsolete; your staff may not know how to use it effectively when you get it; and finally the school board that has been asking for changes to improve the curriculum might not approve the amount of money needed to implement such a program thoughout the district.

There are some things you can do and approaches you can follow to minimize a few of these problems. If you follow the systematic program planning and development outlined in these chapters you will have an idea of your real needs, objectives, and strategies for improving your instructional programs. This can provide the basis for evaluating the effectiveness of any equipment system in contributing to the achievement of your goals, rather than someone else's experiences or the manufacturer's brochure. Incorporating the system into a coordinated plan will also ensure that adequate and appropriate software will be provided, inservice training for users conducted, and the time and place of use of the system will be related to the curriculum plan. A cost effectiveness analysis on a program basis, rather than dividing the price by a vague number of children served, will be feasible.

A pilot approach may also be used to permit an in-depth assessment on a trial basis before ordering larger amounts of equipment for district use. This may be done in one school or even one classroom, using the available children as a sample for measuring effectiveness. While this approach may or may not be a sound research design with significant findings, it will permit process and procedure analysis on the best and most efficient use of the system and offer an inservice training opportunity for the staff. Be sure to build enough time into your plan for using a pilot approach to permit this sort of assessment and training. For major equipment systems, one year as a pilot would be a minimum. Remember too that many pilot programs burn brightly for a short time and then flicker out and fade away due to a lack of continuity, planning, and commitment. A pilot program conducted as a part of a planned program for curriculum improvement should include the requirement for a program plan and proposal to implement the innovation districtwide if warranted by the findings of the pilot phase. This should be done concomitantly with the pilot program. The recommendations for implementation should accompany the report of findings.

Costly technological changes, like costly school buildings or furnishings, may have to be phased in over a period of years. If the cost of equipping all your schools with the needed system is prohibitive, phase it in over several years using evaluative input as a corrective factor for each year's program. Another course of action for long-range changes is to introduce the programs for technological innovation into the school district by incorporating them into the planning and construction of new schools. This permits the design of learning spaces and technological systems on a coordinated basis; is an easier bite to manage and evaluate; offers a psychological advantage to a new staff in a new environment; and permits the innovation to take its proper place as an integral part of a schoolwide new instructional program rather than as a limited effort conducted in an otherwise conventional setting.

If your program to improve the curriculum requires major resources for instructional materials, facilities construction, or equipment systems, and your district is willing to make the commitment necessary to support such efforts, develop or seek outside assistance to achieve the capability for making such decisions on the basis of accountability and need. More modest improvement programs will have to rely on the expertise of presently employed staff members. Larger school districts may obtain the full-time services of an educational technologist and materials specialist whose responsibilities can include:

(1) Identifying the technological and material needs of the system he serves.
(2) Translating these needs into meaningful specifications.
(3) Conducting pilot programs, feasibility studies, and evaluations.
(4) Keeping abreast of the latest research and developments.
(5) Providing consultant services to all managers in the system.
(6) Serving as a mediator between educators and the industry producing and marketing instructional materials and equipment.

Medium-sized school districts should look for these capabilities in the leadership of their media services programs or consider the services of a qualified consultant when major decisions are involved. Smaller districts might provide for the training of an existing staff member or request help from the state departments of education or universities.

SUGGESTED SOURCES OF INFORMATION

Educational Technology, 140 Sylvan Avenue, Englewood Cliffs, New Jersey 07632. A monthly journal oriented toward the systematic management of change in education.
Educational Facilities Laboratories, 477 Madison Avenue, New York, N.Y.

10022. For information on educational facilities planning and furnishing.

Audiovisual Instruction, 1201 Sixteenth Street, N.W., Washington, D.C. 20036. Monthly journal of the Association for Educational Communications and Technology (AECT).

Association for Educational Communication and Technology (AECT), 1201 Sixteenth Street, N.W., Washington, D.C. 20036. Membership offers information on media, materials, staff development programs, and a subscription to *Audiovisual Instruction*.

National Association of Educational Broadcasters (NAEB), 1346 Connecticut Avenue, N.W., Washington, D.C. 20036. Membership offers information and publications on educational broadcasting services, programs, and materials.

13

Evaluating the Curriculum Improvement Plan

This chapter provides a broad overview for planning and implementing an evaluation strategy to assess the effectiveness of your curriculum improvement plan. It assumes that the reader is an experienced school administrator with basic knowledge related to conducting educational evaluations and that as an administrator he has access to staff members who can assist him in implementing a total evaluation plan for the school and/or school system. This chapter will not attempt to provide a comprehensive step-by-step procedure for developing an evaluation strategy, but it will provide a basic framework for administrators to consider in planning and implementing a total evaluation plan.

This chapter considers three major areas:

(1) *The relationship between accountability and evaluation,* which offers a brief description of the need for evaluation and its relationship to accountability in education.
(2) *The theory of evaluation,* which provides a conceptual framework for developing an evaluation strategy for a school and/or school system.
(3) *The practice of evaluation,* which illustrates how the theory of evaluation can be implemented in a school and/or school system.

THE RELATIONSHIP BETWEEN ACCOUNTABILITY AND EVALUATION

Today, evaluation is among the administrator's most urgent and difficult problems. This is caused by a renewed emphasis on accountability in education and the numerous changes in instructional goals, objectives, programs, procedures, and practices that are currently sweeping our nation's schools. More often than not, accountability is considered in the narrower sense of assessment and measurement, rather than in its broader and more definitive meaning of being responsible. Accountability demands responsibility.

In education, accountability means that administrators must be responsible to parents for how effectively their children are being taught and to taxpayers for how usefully their money is being spent to improve instructional programs and practices for children. It also refers to responsibility within the educational community. The board of education and the superintendent are not only responsible to the public for achieving predetermined program goals and objectives, but they are also responsible for delivering the necessary supplies, equipment, administrative support, and know-how to school personnel so that they may accomplish their tasks. Program managers are accountable for support to their administrative and supervisory staff, principals and teachers, as well as to the superintendent for producing program results. Principals are accountable to teachers and to the administration; teachers are accountable to the pupils they are teaching. Central office support personnel are responsible for providing goods and services and are, therefore, accountable to principals and teachers. Accountability must be perceived as a two-way street that involves *all individuals* in the total educational system.

Accountability in a system or a school requires that administrators and other personnel have access to relevant planning and evaluation information because program decisions must be made at different levels in the educational system. Those individuals who support and manage school systems or schools must be responsible for educational evaluations that ensure:

(1) That program evaluation information is as good as it can be.
(2) That program evaluation information is limited to findings supported by data.

(3) That evaluation information is used in some systematic fashion so that more efficient and effective means of improving the quality of instruction for children results.

A THEORY OF EVALUATION

The major failing of evaluation stems from the lack of an adequate definition. Past definitions of evaluation have either equated it with measurement and testing, statements of congruence between performance and objectives, or professional judgments relative to program adequacy. None of these definitions is sufficient to provide all the necessary information or to include the multiplicity of activities now regarded as evaluation.

In recent years, there has been a developing definition of evaluation which views evaluation information as vital to the decision-making process. Evaluation strategy based on this definition of evaluation evolves from the following assumptions:

(1) The quality of instructional programs depends upon the quality of decisions made about the instructional programs.
(2) The quality of decisions depends upon the administrator's ability to identify alternatives which comprise decision situations, and to make sound judgments concerning these alternatives.
(3) Making sound judgments requires timely access to valid and reliable information pertaining to alternatives.
(4) Availability of such information requires a systematic means to provide it.
(5) The processes necessary for providing this information for decision-making comprise the concept of evaluation.

The superintendent should base his plan for evaluation on these assumptions or develop a set for his district.

In this conceptual framework, evaluation is viewed as analysis for the improvement of instructional programs rather than as negative criticism of programs. Accepting the assumption that the purpose of evaluation is to provide information for decision-making, it becomes necessary to know what decision situations must be served. There are four educational decisions that need to be considered in assessing an instructional program:

(1) *Planning decisions* are those which focus on needed improvements by specifying the area, major goals, and specific objectives to be served.
(2) *Programming decisions* are those which specify procedures, personnel, facilities, budget, and time requirements for implementing planned activities.
(3) *Implementing decisions* are those in directing programmed activities.
(4) *Program improvement (recycling) decisions* are those including terminating, continuing, evolving or modifying activities.

(5) Decisions about evaluation

Given four kinds of education decisions that need to be considered, there are also four kinds of evaluation strategies: (1) need and feasibility evaluation, (2) input evaluation, (3) process evaluation, and (4) product evaluation. These four evaluation strategies can be summarized as follows:

(1) *Need and feasibility evaluation* consists of defining the environment where change is to occur, the unmet needs, problems underlying those needs, and opportunities for change.
(2) *Input evaluation* consists of identifying and assessing relevant capabilities, strategies which may be appropriate for meeting program goals, and designs which may be appropriate for achieving specific objectives.
(3) *Process evaluation* consists of detecting or predicting defects in the procedural design or its implementation during the implementation stages.
(4) *Product evaluation* consists of determining the effectiveness of the project after it has run full cycle by measuring and interpreting outcomes as they are related to need and feasibility, input, and process.

Components of the Evaluation Design

After the evaluator has selected which of these evaluation strategies are to be used (a total evaluation cycle normally includes all of them), he must plan in detail for designing and implementing the evaluation. This plan should include the following components:

(1) *Delineation of Evaluation*
   - Identify the major level(s) of decision-making to be served: e.g., teacher, program specialist, principal, area superintendent, superintendent, or other.
   - Project the decision situations to be served for each level of decision-making and describe each one in terms of its locus, focus, timing, and composition of alternatives.
   - Define criteria for each decision situation by specifying variables for measurement and standards for use in the judgment of alternatives.
   - Define policies within which the evaluation must operate.

(2) *Collection of Information*
   - Specify the sources of information to be collected.
   - Specify the instruments and methods for collecting the needed information.
   - Specify the sampling procedure to be employed.
   - Specify the conditions and schedule for information to be collected.

(3) *Organization of Information*
   - Specify a format for the information which is to be collected.
   - Specify a means for coding, organizing, storing, and retrieving information.

(4) *Analysis of Information*
   - Specify the analytical procedures to be employed.
   - Specify a means for performing the analysis.

(5) *Reporting of Information*
   - Define the audiences for the evaluation reports.
   - Specify means for providing information to the audiences.
   - Specify the format for evaluation reports and/or reporting sessions.
   - Schedule the reporting of information.

(6) *Administration of the Evaluation*
   - Summarize the evaluation schedule.
   - Define staff and resource requirements and plans for meeting these requirements.
   - Specify means for meeting policy requirements for conduct of the evaluation.
   - Evaluate the potential of the evaluation design for providing information which is valid, reliable, credible, and timely.
   - Specify and schedule means for periodic revision and updating of the evaluation design.
   - Develop a budget for the total evaluation program.

Each of the preceding six major categories in developing and implementing an evaluation design could be explained in greater detail; however, this should suffice to indicate that the design and analysis of educational evaluation is a most complex and difficult undertaking. An example of the application of this evaluation theory to a hypothetical program for ninth and tenth grade underachieving students is presented in the following section.

THE PRACTICE OF EVALUATION

Fairfax County, Virginia, has been one of the fastest growing counties in the nation and is one of the largest school systems in the United States. Realizing the need to develop its educational research, planning, and development capacities in order to deal with the rapid changes in the county, the school system sought and received a Title III Elementary and Secondary Education Act planning grant to identify educational and cultural needs, and to design programs to meet these needs. Developing from the planning project was the Center for Effecting Educational Change (CEEC). CEEC's purposes were to analyze needs, design programs to meet the needs, conduct pilot studies of the designed programs, supervise implementation of operating programs, and to develop and provide continuing evaluation.

The Systematic Change Procedure

Basic to CEEC's purposes was the task of developing and initiating a systematic change procedure for introducing and implementing new programs in county schools. The systematic change procedure implied evaluation at each step in the planning and implementation of a school program. To that end, an evaluation model known as SPEC (Systematic Process for Evaluating Change) was developed by the CEEC staff.

SPEC represents a simplified systems approach to problem solving, advancing the idea that education can be viewed as a system and that the function of evaluation is to make the total system mesh in a smooth, orderly, efficient, and effective manner.

Application of the Model

To illustrate operational phases of the SPEC model in a school program, a hypothetical project follows. This illustration is not intended to be comprehensive in its design.

Project: *A Nongraded Program for Underachievers in Grades 9 and 10*

The basic idea for the project may be generated by teachers, community representatives, administrators, supervisors, or consultants as a result of imaginative thinking, group discussions, inservice programs, research findings from comparable programs, or other related activities. It is essential at this stage that the evaluation process be viewed as a collaborative effort by teachers, administrators, supervisors, and/or consultants.

In our hypothetical case, teachers and administrators in a school have suggested that certain pupils in grades nine and ten were not being reached through the traditional curriculum. A nongraded program, designed for the level of these pupils, has been discussed by the faculty and it appears that this idea should be explored in depth. What guidelines can be followed in introducing, implementing, and evaluating such a new program? Figure 13-1 summarizes application of the SPEC model for evaluating the nongraded program.

According to the systematic change procedure, *need and feasibility* evaluation conducted by local school and central office personnel should be initiated to: define the types and kinds of courses or programs now being offered to these students; determine if such courses or programs are needed; assess the local school and school system data on standardized achievement, intelligence, and aptitude tests that are available; assess information available from the school, home, community, parents, pupils, and teachers; evaluate existing local and national research that is similar or related; determine the feasibility of conducting the program in terms of available human and material resources, organization, training, inservice provisions, and other similar considerations; identify the problems underlying the needs; and determine how the project will be developed to contribute to the

THE SYSTEMATIC PROCESS FOR EVALUATING CHANGE
"SPEC" EVALUATION MODEL

Evaluation Component	Identification of Information Needs	Criteria for Decision	Data Collection	Data Organization	Data Analysis	Reporting
Need and Feasibility To identify and assess deficiencies in educational opportunities	Current status of program or status requiring program	Significant disparity between status and norms or desired mastery level	census data	manual computer •general and special programs	statistical analysis content analysis depth study	formal reports •written •tabular informal reports
	Current status of human and material resources		demographic study			
	Status of school program		standardized tests		case study	•group •individual
	Socio-economic status		pupil grades			
	Norms desired		pupil attendance			
	Mastery desired		dropout data			
			attitude survey			
			questionnaires			
			locally constructed tests			

Figure 13-1

Evaluation Component	Identification of Information Needs	Criteria for Decision	Data Collection	Data Organization	Data Analysis	Reporting
Input To identify and assess designs and strategies for program	Relationship of program to total educational program Data on previous programs or similar programs Available solutions to the problem	Feasibility validity barriers tension cost-effectiveness	Review of literature Interviews with school personnel, experts, community leaders, and parents Panels, seminars, group meetings Transfer from other Title I or III programs Observation of demonstrations	manual computer •general and special programs	statistical analysis of cost case study consultants for feasibility, barriers, and tension Educational Team Approach analysis for validity	formal reports •written •tabular informal reports •group •individual

Figure 13-1 (Continued)

Evaluation Component	Identification of Information Needs	Criteria for Decision	Data Collection	Data Organization	Data Analysis	Reporting
Process To identify and assess the program design and procedures	Barriers to success interaction problems inter and intra problems problem areas progress areas	acceptability utilization integration assimilation	curriculum information (materials) operation and management information logs observation interviews (group and individual) inservice meetings other instruments: •attitude •acceptance •questionnaire •other	manual computer •general and special programs	content analysis statistical analysis	formal reports •written •tabular informal reports •group •individual

Figure 13-1 (Continued)

Evaluation Component	Identification of Information Needs	Criteria for Decision	Data Collection	Data Organization	Data Analysis	Reporting
Product To measure the outcomes of the program in relation to objectives	project outcomes •achievement •attitude •curriculum developed •operation and management procedures •cost-effectiveness	achievement desired growth desired attitude desired curriculum desired	standardized tests pupil grades attitude scale attendance level dropout rate locally constructed test	manual computer •general and special programs	statistical analysis pre-post experimental-control content analysis population analysis accounting	formal reports •written •tabular •statistical informal reports •group •individual •statistical dissemination of reports

Figure 13-1 (Continued)

school system as well as to the local school. Together, these assessment procedures constitute need and feasibility evaluation.

Input evaluation involves utilizing supervisors, consultants, and subject matter personnel from various sources who can formulate potential solutions to the problem. These potential solutions should be viewed in reference to barriers (such as acceptance of the solution by teachers and students); workability (possible operation of the proposed solution in the class or school); sufficiency (ability of solutions to overcome the problem or educational deficiency), and the economic cost (relationship of costs of proposed solutions to expected educational gains). Input evaluation leads to the development of various strategies and procedures, and information becomes available for deciding which strategy and procedure should be employed. In addition, input evaluation identifies the potential problem areas to be monitored during the implementation.

Process evaluation is the information management system for decisions concerning the expansion, contraction, modification and clarification of the solution strategy. The local school staff plays the most important role in this process because it monitors the design and procedure of the program and provides information on the events and activities of the program. This information allows *changes to be made* while the program is in process, a prerequisite to ensuring successful program implementation.

Product evaluation consists of the more traditional measurement which relates outcomes of the program to objectives. The variables tested are dependent upon objectives such as achievement of pupils, improved attitudes of students toward subject matter areas, improved school holding-power, improved attendance, impact on other subject areas, and other variables that can be expected to change.

These are but some of the uses of the components of evaluation. Often, the limitations of time, personnel, and other resources make it impossible to implement a comprehensive evaluation design such as that presented in this chapter. In this case, the program administrator must select the most important aspects of the project for intensive evaluation in order to provide the essential information for decision-making and program improvement. To summarize, the SPEC model is a general framework for the evaluation of change. It is a systems approach to change, designed to provide information for sound decision-making.

14

Quality Education Through Continuous Curriculum Improvement

The educational planner responsible for providing quality education must have a rationale for identifying and defining "quality education." He may turn to the literature for a ready-made definition (and such definitions are available for the asking) or he may seek to develop his own definition based upon a determination of goals appropriate to the clientele to be served. This book has explored the latter approach aiming specifically at curriculum improvement for elementary and secondary schools.

CRITERIA FOR EVALUATING A PROGRAM
OF QUALITY EDUCATION

Education is quality education to the extent that it meets the needs of the students being served and to the extent that it helps solve their problems and fosters their optimum growth and development. It is seldom a readily identifiable combination of learning activities directly measurable by qualitative and quantitative criteria. It is more a direction than a destination, and there is no magic point at which a program suddenly becomes a quality program. There is some quality in the poorest program, and no program is without some non-quality components.

Within this broad context, it is possible to identify certain hallmarks of quality education, certain supporting elements that are essential to and characteristic of an educational program achieving this desired goal. These include adequate financial support, teachers trained for specific tasks, liberal allowances for teaching supplies and materials, accredited schools, flexible organizational patterns, and modern, well-equipped buildings. All of these must be taken into account by the educational planner as he develops a strategy for providing quality education. However, they do not guarantee a quality program in and of themselves.

Quality education in a given educational enterprise (be it a school district, a school, or a class) must be operated to provide the activities necessary to meet the needs of students and should be undertaken in two distinct phases: (1) an analysis of the general characteristics of the group and community being served, and (2) an analysis of the characteristics and needs of each individual within the group. The first includes items about the community served: its ethnic origins, its attitude toward and willingness to support education, its educational goals, its income level, its employment opportunities, its educational level, and similar demographic data. These data provide the broad constraints within which key administrators or other educational planners must develop the school program. They determine where emphasis should be placed, identify where compensatory educational opportunities should be offered, and identify the general tone that a school must take. They will identify needs that the planner sees as opportunities for educational improvement. To the extent that the program provides for these needs, quality education exists.

The program planner must have an intimate knowledge and understanding of the population to be served if he is to be effective in identifying the overall needs of the group and of each individual within that group. Many resources are available to the planner as he undertakes such an assessment. Much of the statistical data is available from other agencies and from members of the school staff. Surveys, observations, simple questionnaires, and an analysis of pupil performance can contribute heavily to this analysis. Involvement of students and parents in this activity is essential and highly desirable.

An analysis of the needs of each individual pupil and a program for meeting his unique needs are critical parts of any quality education program. The characteristics and needs of each pupil can be assessed through tests, observations, counseling, and consultation. In addition to the traditional aptitude and achievement scores, special interests, skills, talents, and handicaps should be noted. The fostering of an attitude of respect for the worth and dignity of each individual should be an important by-product of this process.

Once both group and individual needs are identified, they should become the bases for program planning and evaluation. To the extent that the current program meets these needs, it is a quality program. Unmet needs indicate ground yet to be covered and provide the thrusts for educational renovation and improvement. The evaluation of the program should then be based upon performance indicators that are related to identified pupil needs. 'For example: paucity of dropouts rather than size of guidance departments becomes a quality measure, ability of youngsters to read becomes a quality measure rather than the number of remedial reading teachers, and youngsters learning through self-direction and self-discipline rather than lower pupil-teacher ratios becomes a measure of quality.

In summary, this two-part assessment should: (1) identify what the population is like, as a group and as individuals; (2) determine their needs based upon these characteristics and the goals established for the educational enterprise; (3) identify which of these needs are currently being met; and (4) identify those needs not currently being met. Meeting the remaining needs provides the thrust toward quality education.

CONSIDERATIONS FOR THE EDUCATIONAL PLANNER
AS HE SEEKS IMPROVEMENT

The identification of what quality education is, and how much farther the program will have to go (and many schools and school systems are either unable or unwilling to submit their program to such an analysis), represents the first step in developing the desired programs and effecting the desired changes.

Following the identification of needs, programs of learning experiences should be developed aimed at meeting these needs. The planner must draw upon all available resources in developing these programs. Seldom is he able to attack all needs with sufficient resources to ensure a reasonable degree of success in all. Priorities will have to be established and the less critical needs deferred or postponed. Resources at his disposal include his own experience and expertise, and the expertise of members of his staff, outside consultants, parents, community leaders, and students. A careful review of the research and literature in the field may prevent the duplication of mistakes made elsewhere, or prevent the planner from "reinventing the wheel." As a planning team composed of some combination of these resources moves toward the implementation of a new or revised program, there are a number of specific questions that should be carefully considered.

First, is the program feasible? Are the finances, personnel, instructional materials, facilities, and orientation adequate in quantity and quality to ensure a reasonable chance of success? Funds must be available to provide the resources necessary to support the program. Obviously a program with a per pupil cost of $100,000 would seldom, if ever, be feasible even if success were guaranteed. However, the planner must not assume that an educational improvement is possible only when additional funds are available. Each program planner should explore the possibility of reallocating existing resources and/or deleting an existing resource before assuming automatically that he must have additional support to introduce a new program. A budget preparation document should provide the flexibility necessary to make reallocation of existing resources a prerequisite to the request for new resources. (In fact, the program budgeting request form for the Fairfax County Public Schools makes provision for requesting reallocation of existing funds, materials, and finances as a prelude to requesting additional program funds.)

Once financial feasibility is established, the planner should ascertain that facilities can be made available, that personnel can be obtained, that required course outlines and guides will be ready, that the administrative organization will foster rather than restrict the program, and that a climate has been developed in which the program will receive a fair shake. In practice, this model is seldom completely attainable, but the planner should aim for this ideal. Probably more educational innovations and renovations have failed to produce desired results because of poor planning and lack of support than because of basic weaknesses in the programs themselves. It is frequently wiser to postpone the change until support is adequate.

Only when the planner has determined that the resources and support will be available should he move to implement the program. If, as is usually the case, more than one approach to the program appears to hold promise, he should (to the extent possible) test alternate approaches, identifying in advance some way to assess the relative success of each approach.

Continuous evaluation of the program is essential and should be an integral part of the planning-implementation process. The evaluation design should include an identification of objectives of the program, an identification of the activities through which they will be attained, and a scheme for identifying to what extent the objectives are attained. Evaluation should measure the changes in student achievement and behavior, because these changes are central to the purpose of the program. However, the full potential of the evaluative process is realized only if it assesses the relative effectiveness of the various techniques and materials and the appropriateness of the objectives themselves. In so doing, the evaluation provides the planner with insights for improving the program.

In effect, the program planner identifies the needs of students, plans a program based upon these needs, includes activities to meet these needs, plans adequately to provide necessary resources, evaluates carefully, and recommends and introduces improvements based upon this evaluation. It would seem that this approach could hardly be questioned and that such a plan would receive the unqualified plaudits of students, parents, and fellow educators. Experience indicates that this is not always the case. Although a plan such as that outlined (or some similar systematic approach to change) is essential to widespread acceptance of an educational change, it does not automatically guarantee smooth implementation.

There are certain additional considerations that any educational planner, but particularly the key administrator, must take into account if he introduces educational changes that will provide quality education for his students. Some of the more crucial, presented in outline form, are as follows:

(1) Unless the planner is committed to the change, he should not undertake it.

(2) All persons affected by the change should be involved—both those who will participate and benefit from it and those who feel threatened and may lose status from it. This includes students, parents, teachers, supervisors, and administrators.

(3) Delineation of responsibility must be clearly established. Possible friction points must be identified in advance, and responsibility, together with the authority necessary to carry out this responsibility, must be carefully spelled out.

(4) The decision-making process must be clearly defined as to when and by whom decisions will be made. It should force a review, making a "desk top" veto impossible.

(5) There must be a districtwide commitment to the change, but especially from the key administrator and school board. It must include a commitment of people, time, funds, and logistic support, not just a "go ahead and try it, we're behind you."

(6) The planner must identify in realistic terms the support that he needs. He should never, in his enthusiasm to get going, agree to implement a program without adequate support.

(7) Change cannot be effected as a part-time, after hours, Monday faculty-meeting-only, enterprise. Resources, funds, and time must be provided for the planning phases.

(8) There must be a willingness on the part of the planner and his staff to depart from existing patterns, to run the risk of failure and to be criticized for being dreamers on the one hand and for not doing enough on the other.

(9) The planner must identify key people who can either facilitate the desired improvement or can block its effectiveness. Within the school district, these persons may be either in the informal power structure or identifiable on the organization chart. They also include board members, citizens, and students.

(10) It must be recognized that budget time and the budget process are critical to program implementation. Timing, justification, and planning must take this into account.

THE QUEST FOR EDUCATIONAL QUALITY

The key administrator, to provide quality education for the students of his school or district, must work continually with all appropriate groups to bring about an awareness of the need for and a tolerance toward educational change and improvement. He must become a manager of educational resources, not just an assigner of principals and teachers. He must identify new roles for himself, his staff, the community, and the students. He must remain aware of emerging trends in education and function in the total environment of the community.

The quest for educational quality through bringing about educational improvements is an exciting, rewarding, but, at the same time, frustrating job. The role of the key administrator has always been that of change agent. He has grappled with the quest for quality for years, often finding it postponed as he struggled to meet day-to-day emergencies. It seems almost presumptuous to suggest that he consider seriously what has been said in the pages of this book. Yet, many key administrators have implemented systematic program change, some with even greater depth and with greater intensity than suggested here. Educational leadership will continue to be a meaningful, professionally rewarding experience only to the extent that there continues to be a quest for quality education that will meet the needs of the students that are to be served.

SELECTED REFERENCES FOR ADDITIONAL READING

Alexander, William M. (ed.) *The Changing Secondary School Curriculum.* New York: Holt, Rinehart and Winston, 1967.

Bagin, Donald L., Frank Grazian and Charles H. Harrison. *School Communications: Ideas That Work.* New York: McGraw-Hill Book Company, Inc., 1972.

Bloom, Benjamin S., J. Thomas Hastings, and George F. Madans. *Handbook on Formative and Summative Evaluation of Student Learning.* New York: McGraw-Hill Book Company, 1971.

Bortner, Doyle M. *Public Relations for Public Schools.* Cambridge, Mass.: Schenkman Publishing Co., 1972.

Communicating Ideas in Action. Washington, D.C.: National School Public Relations Association, 1970.

Cook, Desmond. *Program Evaluation and Review Technique: Applications in Education.* U.S. Office of Education, Cooperative Research Monograph No. 17, OE-12024. Washington, D.C.: U.S. Government Printing Office, 1966.

Ellena, William J. (ed.). *Curriculum Handbook for School Executives.* Arlington, Virginia: American Association of School Administrators, 1973.

Evaluation Instrument for Educational Public Relations Programs. Washington, D.C.: National School Public Relations Association, 1972.

Garvue, Robert J. *Modern Public School Finance.* Toronto, Ontario: The Macmillan Company, 1969.

Hartley, Harry J. *Educational Planning-Programming-Budgeting: A Systems Approach.* Englewood Cliffs, N.J.: Prentice-Hall, Inc., 1968.

Kaufman, Roger A. *Educational System Planning.* Englewood Cliffs., N.J.: Prentice-Hall, Inc., 1972.

Knezevich, Stephen J. (ed.). *Administrative Technology and the School Executive.* Washington, D.C.: American Association of School Administrators, 1969.

Leeper, Robert R. (ed.). *Strategy for Curriculum Change.* Washington, D.C.: Association for Supervision and Curriculum Development, 1965.

Levin, Sol. *PPBS in Public Education: A Manual for School Administrators and Board Members.* Swarthmore, Pa.: A.C. Craft, Inc., 1971.

Mager, Robert F. *Preparing Instructional Objectives.* Palo Alto, Calif.: Fearon Publishers, Inc., 1962.

McManama, John. *Systems Analysis for Effective School Administration.* West Nyack, New York: Parker Publishing Company, Inc., 1971.

Phi Delta Kappa National Study Committees on Evaluation. *Educational Evaluation and Decision Making.* Itasca, Ill.: F.E. Peacock Publishers, Inc., 1971.

Provus, Malcolm. *Discrepancy Evaluation for Educational Program Improvement and Assessment.* Berkeley, Calif.: McCutchan Publishing Corporation, 1971.

Putting Words and Pictures About Schools Into Print. Washington, D.C.: National School Public Relations Association, 1971.

Saylor, J. Galen and William M. Alexander. *Curriculum Planning for Modern Schools.* New York: Holt, Rinehart and Winston, Inc., 1966.

Tyler, Ralph W., Robert M. Gagne, and Michael Scriven. *Perspectives of Curriculum Evaluation,* AERA Monograph Series on Curriculum Evaluation 1. Chicago: Rand McNally and Company, 1967.

Wiles, Kimball. *The Changing Curriculum of the American High School.* Englewood Cliffs, N.J.: Prentice-Hall, Inc., 1963.

Wilhelms, Fred T. (ed.). *Evaluation as Feedback and Guide.* Washington, D.C.: Association for Supervision and Curriculum Development, 1967.

Wynne, Edward. *The Politics of School Accountability: Public Information About Public Schools.* Berkeley, Calif.: McCutchan Publishing Corporation, 1972.

Index

205